Creating a Country Inn

Creating a Country Inn

WILLIAM CASSILL

Alpharetta, GA

ISBN: 978-1-63183-034-1

10 9 8 7 6 5 4 3 2 0 8 2 6 1 6

Printed in the United States of America

∞This paper meets the requirements of ANSI/NISO Z39.48-1992 (Permanence of Paper)

Acknowledgement

There were many people that had a share in making the Inn happen. Starting with the first person we met on our initial look at this wonderful property: Dave Berrie, Ed Druke, Amon DeWitt, Bill Cobb, Gene Garbe, Jane St.Pierre, Bob St.Pierre. Randi Powling, Cindy Berrie, Jessica Slowik, Molly Melloan, Fred Houston, Jacques Allembert, and Dr. Robert Backus.

Of course, the family involvement was very important to us: Jon Cassill, and Laurie and Darren Keefe.

Thanks to Jon for his advice and help with colors, wall paper, painting of our bedroom mural, and for the drawing of our Inn that you see in this memoir. Thank you, Laurie for being so very helpful with renovation projects and managing the completion of projects while caring for our house during the two years Mom and I spent in England. And, of course, for helping when we needed you. Thanks to Darren for working directly with us, and giving us solid support, over the more than four years we operated our Inn.

My writing of this memoir would not be complete without acknowledging the importance of my writer friend and volunteer editor. Virginia Hicks has made more contributions to this than anyone will realize. I sincerely thank her for her critiques and grammatical suggestions.

Writing this memoir would not have been possible without Sandra, my wife and co-Inn Keeper. Her involvement and care in creating the Country Inn at Williamsville, Vermont was both physical and spiritual. It was totally challenging and she stuck with it the entire way. It could not and would not have been done without her.

Contents

Introduction

This memoir is from a period of dramatic change in life style . . . a change to a totally new way of life. The change involved a move from an executive management position and international travel, to an early 1800's era farm in Vermont. This is about taking on the challenge of creating a totally new Country Inn while working within a cumbersome Vermont State regulatory process, and building a new life involving financial challenge and the interest of the Internal Revenue Service.

There were many steps to be taken, leading us, the author and my wife, through an extensive renovation to the opening and operation of our Inn. The thirteen year period began with the New York Times classified advertising that led to our new life, and ended with our last involvement in the property that had become a Vermont Country Inn. This story allows the expression of this part of our life, and answers many requests and questions.

Frequently, when new acquaintances are told of our past Inn Keeper life, we hear the question: "Oh, I/We have always wanted to do that. What was it like?" The answer is here. These pages cover the progress of our decision to buy, to renovate and modernize, and the opening and operation of our Inn. We learned from our experience, and I have included some rules and tips from our perspective of this Inn life. I believe this will be helpful to readers who may be giving serious consideration to Inn Keeping, or may just be curious about what it was like.

I hope you may find this interesting. Our involvement with the land and the house, and then with the guests and the business, made a very personally rewarding and satisfying life for us. Good Luck to you!

The Beginning

My wife, Sandra, and I, were living in Connecticut in a condominium home near the Long Island Sound, with an easy walk to the beach, tennis and golf. In short, we were in an enviable position. I had a good, if demanding, job. Sandra had volunteer activities. We both had a strong circle of friends with social and intellectual friendships.

This was a Sunday afternoon. We had been discussing the trip we would be taking to attend a wedding in northern Vermont. Two of our best and long-time friends were away on a long business assignment in Kenya, and would not be able to make it back for their daughter's wedding. They had made the decision to stay in Kenya, and use the money to bring the bride and groom for a honeymoon visit to Kenya, which would probably be a once-in-a lifetime opportunity for the couple.

We had known the daughter since Sandra was her Sunday school teacher, and felt it very important to be there for the wedding as a gift to our friends. This would be a two day trip and would give us some time for touring. The weather would be ideal, as it was July in Vermont. Our many previous Vermont visits had always been for skiing, so this would be our first summer time trip.

After we finished the trip planning, I sat down with the Sunday New York Times. As was my normal routine, I picked up the real estate section to browse. This time I was immediately drawn to the country properties and my attention fixed on Vermont. There was a classified ad that described a property purporting to be a location of more than 100 acres, with house and barn perfect for a country inn or horse farm. The price seemed reasonable.

This created more than a casual reaction. After all we had decided on the wedding trip to Vermont. Why not tie in a stop to see this property? Over the course of several years, since we had begun skiing as adults, the idea of a Vermont property had semi-lodged in my head. Perhaps, we could consider something like this for an early retirement. Sandra thought it a good idea that we stop to look, since we were taking the trip. A telephone call to the realtor's number set up an appointment for a visit on the return trip from the wedding.

The day of the wedding was idyllic. Weather was perfect. On the drive north through Vermont, we stopped to eat a picnic lunch in a small town, home to a college. After eating the lunch Sandra had packed, I dozed under a large tree. Sandra took a short walk pursuing the piano music she heard playing from the college. This was a wonderful start for the rest of the trip.

The wedding was set outdoors near a stream at the home of the groom. As we pulled up to the home of the groom's parents, the groom dressed in a formal white tuxedo was directing traffic for parking. The bride was beautiful in her long-white gown, and the ceremony was held under an arbor, built especially for the occasion. The wedding ceremony was highlighted by classical music interspersed with birds singing in the surrounding trees. The reception, featuring music from the fiddle of the groom's father, was the perfect end to the romantic day.

The next day was back to southern Vermont, where we met the Realtor, Dave Berrie, for a tour of the property. The farm house and property were no longer actively occupied. It was owned by two couples, who used this as a vacation and holiday location for their families. The families were now all grown and used it infrequently. With the local realtor serving as guide, we learned the house had been built in three parts; the first smaller part in the late 1700s, the main part circa 1830 with some add-on in the 1960s.

The farm was no longer operated, but it had been an active dairy farm up until the end of World War II. At that time the federal-style home and lands were purchased by a successful New York banker and his sister as a retirement home. They did extensive remodeling and brought the home into the Twentieth Century. Among all their improvements, they introduced interior bathrooms, brought electrical wiring up to code, modernized the heating system, and provided running water. They replaced powder post beetle-eaten support beams and removed some of the interior walls to give more expansive living spaces on the first floor.

We were told the previous owners, who had completed the modernization, passed away in the early 1960s. The property was purchased by the two current owners and their wives to serve as a vacation home for their children and their friends. They had added more space to the home by closing in the horse and carriage barn, and attaching it to the rear of the oldest part of the original house. This was then made into a large recreation area with office and storage area. The second floor was made into bedrooms with a spiral staircase down to the rec room.

As we explored, we found the ten bedrooms and three bathrooms on the second floor. We were told the owners frequently had twenty or more young guests; but it was obvious, that if we were going to develop this into a country inn, we would need to add more private baths. That, of course, would mean remodeling, which would reduce the number of bedrooms. There would be other significant considerations, but we didn't have the time now for the required depth of evaluation. We still had to see the barn across the road and wanted to see the fields and bordering river, before heading back to Connecticut.

Stepping out of the front door, the view across the narrow road was particularly charming. The large red barn with its high gambrel roof and attached silo was straight out of a classical Currier and Ives print. Next to the barn, the lush green grass led to the edge of a large pond with massive willow trees. Beyond the pond, we could see hay fields with the uncut hay waving gently in the summer breezes. Completing this idyllic view, the fields led to a low mountain range, which the Realtor explained, started to rise slowly beyond the river that marked the boundary of this property.

The Realtor told us that the source of the pond's fresh water was the year-round flow of water from springs dotting the wooded hillside above the farm house. The springs also fed a stream that flowed downhill until it reached a culvert, where it passed under the road before continuing on down to the river. This lower part of the stream, down to the river, would only flow during snow melt high water time in the spring. The upper part of the stream flowed year round and went underground near the road, where it fed an ingenious system of pipes that had been dug years ago and provided the fresh water to the pond. The current owners had excavated the pond to deepen it, and had stocked the pond with both rainbow and brown trout.

We crossed the road and entered the barn, which had not been used for farming since 1945. We could see the long row of cow-milking stanchions that had been left there since the end of World War II, when the dairy farmer stopped his dairy business. There was a ladder going to the second floor, but we decided there wasn't enough time now for investigating upstairs. We walked out the back door to an open storage area under a roof connected to the back wall of the barn. There were several pieces of farming equipment stored here, and the Realtor explained that though they were all old, they were usable and there was everything needed to complete haying the fields.

Time was getting short, so checking out the vast expanse of hay fields or going down to the pond and to the swimming hole at the river would not be possible before we had to leave for the drive home. We did walk to the edge of the fields behind the barn to stand and admire the waving of the hay. It was obvious that it was time for the fields to be cut. What would it be like to see and walk all of this when the paths and the view would be unencumbered by the tall hay?

Time had gone by quickly, and we knew we had to leave for home. We were definitely appreciative of the time the Realtor had spent with us; we expressed our thanks to him and bid him goodbye.

We knew this tour had given us a view of another life and were clearly intrigued by what we had seen. We also knew this trip demanded a return to either get this idea out of our heads or get more serious. Within two weeks we had a trip planned to fly to Seattle to see our daughter, Laurie. We would have some time to continue thinking about this dramatic Vermont undertaking, and could decide if we definitely wanted to come back for another look.

Another Look

Our visit to Seattle was delightful. It was wonderful to see our Laurie, and she had been able to arrange time off and tour with us. She showed us around the city and out in the country for all the touristy things to do. In the short time she had been in Seattle, she had made a number of friends, both young and older, so we were quite pleased with her new life.

Naturally, we told her of our recent Vermont trip and introduced the idea of the potential inn life we were exploring. We treated this as fundamentally casual in our level of discussion, and at that point, beyond the realm of possibility. You know simply, "Dad would take early retirement, we would sell our condo, buy the Vermont property, remodel the old house, and open a country inn. After all, wasn't Bob Newhart planning to open his Vermont Inn on television this fall?" This was all presented in a somewhat humorous fashion, but it did get the idea out on the table. We still had a return trip we should take ,and a lot more thinking about what would be required to actually make such a decision. In any case, it would be another two years before I would be the age of early retirement.

At the end of the week, we finished our lengthy goodbye hugs and boarded our return flight. Our long flight gave us a lot of time to think about this Vermont possibility, and we thought we owed it to ourselves to have another look at the land and the house and barn. We arrived home and called the broker to set up another visit the following weekend.

Saturday morning dawned with clear skies, but we started driving with some degree of apprehension. This possible undertaking would be a truly major change in our life. We had moved many times in my working career, but this would be the first time without the support of my employer. We had a lot to think about on this weekend trip.

We decided to do a drive-by of the property before going to the nearby town to check into the Inn where the Realtor had reserved a room for us. As mentioned earlier, the property was more than 100 acres with a narrow paved Town road splitting the farm into two nearly equal parts. We drove along this road, and clocked the road frontage at nearly 6/10 of a mile in length. The land, where the house and an out-building that served as a garage were located, was the only level piece on the left side of the road; the remainder was nearly all hill. Driving past the house and then a pond, we could see that the land had a rather steep slope going up and away from the road on the left. The right side of the road had a steep drop-off. We had been told we wouldn't be able to see too far into the woods on either side of the road, but knew that on the left it was nearly all woods up to the property line up the hill.

The right side of the road was level for perhaps 400 feet along one of the fields fronting on the road. Continuing on the road just as it began a very gradual up-hill, we came to the barn on the right. We'll talk more of the barn, but it was ideally positioned for easy access to the pond and to the large fields leading down to the river. The pond was positioned across the road from the house and at the base of a steep drop-off from the road. The edge of the road had been planted in times past with what were now giant locust trees that served as sentries to keep careless drivers from going off the road and down the slope into the pond. As the road continued up the hill, the drop-off on the right became steeper and deeper until we reached the property line. Again, because of the woods we could not see the river and swimming hole down below, but we knew it was there and would investigate it later.

This driving look was exciting! For a couple that had never had any personal involvement with land such as this, it was exhilarating especially knowing that we had only seen the edges. This was really the first time the realization of possibly becoming the owners began to strike home. The road leveled off at the top of the hill, and there was a small pull-off area where we stopped to marvel at what we were seeing and feeling.

Anxious to get out of the car and explore on foot, we drove on to the nearby town and checked into the Inn. They were also offering dinner in their well-known dining room, but we had already planned to check out the closest larger town in the area for dinner. We had brought a picnic lunch with us and returned to the pond, where we then had our picnic under one of the huge willow trees. We leaned back against the tree and listened to the peaceful sounds of the birds.

Our realtor,Dave, arrived to begin his guided tour of the outdoor attractions with the promise of additional time back in the house. The first thing he further explained was the pond. This was circular, approximately 1/3 of an acre and was about 12 feet deep at the center. He had explained the water inlet system on the last visit and now showed us the outlet so necessary to keep the water flowing and fresh to sustain the trout. The outlet was a pipe that would take the water overflow deep to a horizontal pipe that provided an outlet to the ground that sloped away. The water would then trickle into a shallow creek bed, then form a small pond from which the water would percolate down through the soil or evaporate into air. This explanation caused us to focus on the fresh country air we were breathing and to realize the health benefits of living in such surroundings.

Our next stop was a short walk into the barn. As we stepped into the barn, we again realized the size of it would allow us to use it for purposes we hadn't even thought about. The first floor was 12 feet high, and after climbing the ladder to the second floor, we found the roof to be 14 feet more. The design of the room was gambrel style so there were no vertical supports. The entirely open expanse gave the impression of a large ballroom. There was a large area of the floor open down to the first so that hay could be easily tossed down for the former cows. This upper floor had an opening to the currently unused silo at one end of the barn. The other end had an opening with a door that would have been used for a hay elevator to move the hay bales as they were brought off the fields to the upper storage floor. We were reminded by our realtor that the barn hadn't been used for any farming activity other than hay storage since 1945.

Stepping out through the back of the barn to look at the fields, we were struck by a huge difference. When we were here three weeks ago the fields had not been hayed. The grasses had been high and were difficult to walk through so we had cut short our efforts to try it. Now, the hay had been mowed, and the feeling was entirely different. Whereas the fields before haying had given a closed in feeling, now there was a sensation of a vast open expanse with freedom to move and do whatever the spirit wished. We moved past some trees that delineated two parts of the larger field and saw a farmer on a tractor down at the end of a field. The Realtor explained that the owners had an arrangement with the farmer who would do the haying and remove the hay for his own use in exchange for mowing.

We walked through the field, and were told that at some time during past millennia these fields would have been part of a glacial lake. As the waters gradually receded, the land formed into a series of plateaus creating three different levels of fields between the river, and up to the paved Town road running through the property. At the lowest level of the field, the river bordered the property for a length of nearly one-half mile. Standing on the edge of the field, as we gazed at the river that August, it was filled with rocks both large and small with the water only inches-deep slowly meandering through them. We were told that in the spring when the water from snow melt is at its highest, the river runs the fastest and roughest. This is the time we may see rough water kayakers riding the flow down the river, aptly named Rock River, for several miles; where it connects with the major West River.

Our walk continued on the lower field along the river where we came upon the highlight of the river. This is the point just short of the property line for the farm and is the base of the rock face coming down from the highest point on this property. Over the centuries, the fast moving spring river flow had bumped up against the rock face causing the river to veer away, carving out a swimming hole nine feet deep with a channel 75 feet long ranging in depth from 3 feet to 9 feet. As it was creating the swimming channel, the river brought in sand developing a small beach of perhaps 150 square feet. To top this off, the high point of the rock face at the river was 10 feet above the deepest part of the swimming area, with a tree and rope attached for swinging into the water. The nicest aspect of this swimming hole is that the water remains deep at this point, even throughout the times of year when the river is shallow, providing a delightfully pleasant swimming experience.

Our interest level and excitement by this time, having viewed the vistas, the pond and river, could not have been at a higher level. We realized we had to see more of the house, so in the time left in the afternoon we headed back to the house. By this time, the house had a familiar feel to it. We began examining the rooms with an idea of how they would work for us if we followed through with the idea of a country inn. Keeping in mind that the house had been drastically renovated by the banker and his sister, we could see that what might have been considered originally as a routine farm house was now something that could work for us.

The large living room that had been created from two smaller rooms had a big fireplace and could be perfect for guest lounging or even weddings. There was a wood-paneled room with built-in book cases and another fireplace. As we continued to look, we found ourselves imagining the other rooms and their uses for dining, kitchen, bedrooms, storage, and anything else we might think of.

In other words we were getting hooked.

We bid Dave goodbye for the day and headed into the nearby town. There was plenty of daylight left to look over the town on this August summer day. It was a half hour drive from the house to major shopping for groceries as well as all the other major shopping requirements. The hospital was also quite modern and had a good reputation. Our looking was mostly drive-by, but from our discussions with the realtor, as well as reference materials he had provided, we had a good understanding of the area. We could see there were several churches, a movie theatre, several restaurants, bars and a micro-brewery. We understood there was a nearby small liberal arts college that provided a classical musical program for seniors several weeks over the summer months. We didn't plan on visiting the downhill ski areas this trip as we had spent many ski weekends and vacations skiing in the area. Mt. Snow was about thirty minutes and Stratton about forty-five minutes away from the farm.

This had been a long and active day, so we found the restaurant that had been suggested by our realtor. We happily settled into our booth, had a glass of wine and studied the menu. We had a lot to talk about over the dinner. We knew we would have to renovate to add bathrooms for each guest room and discussed how that could be done. The recreation room could be converted into a commercial kitchen and the current kitchen could be converted into another dining room. The heating system would have to be changed.

There were other changes we could make, but that was enough for that evening. We made our way back to the Inn and accepted our room key from the Innkeepers. They were curious about our day, but we were not ready at that time to talk about any plans we were thinking about, so we said our goodnights.

Falling In Love

The next morning, we arose, dressed, went downstairs and were greeted by the sight of a nearly full dining room. This sight was extremely charming and we began to better understand the importance of the dining area with its warm atmosphere, the smells from the kitchen, and selections of food to please the palate. This immediately reinforced some of the discussion we had had last evening.

Mind you, we still had not made any decisions, but the hook was being set even deeper.

Following a hearty breakfast, we went back upstairs and packed our light bags. We thanked our Innkeepers for a delightful room and breakfast and checked out, anxious to begin our day of exploring the land further.

Since we had our realtor as tour guide yesterday, we wanted to investigate on our own today. We drove to the house and parked in the driveway. We hadn't planned on visiting inside the house again, but knew that if we changed our minds we could call the realtor and were sure he would accommodate us.

The first thing we did was walk up the hill behind the house into the old apple orchard. We stood above the edge of the hill where the old cider mill had been. This gave us a view over the house looking through the tops of the locust trees lining the road in front of the house. Looking down on the house allowed us to see the L-shape that had not been obvious from our prior views from the front.

As we turned around, we could see just beyond the apple trees a broad expanse of field that ran at a shallow up-hill slope to a tree line. We found what appeared to be an old logging road that was more like a wide path. As we started up this path, suddenly there was a loud noise of fluttering wings. We had startled and flushed two grouse that flew past us into another part of the woods. Needless to say they startled us also. Before we could get deep into the woods, we came upon two separate small spring houses that had been built to protect the sources of the springs that supplied the house with its delicious water. We had been told by the realtor that these two houses were tied into a single 500 foot long pipe that ran down the hill into a cistern in the basement of the house.

As we continued our walk uphill, the trees were mostly pine, and they were immense. When we had first met Dave, he had shown us a brief collection of old photographs that had been taken by a local well known photographer in the early 1900's. He had one photo that was rather striking. It had shown the hillside behind the house, and the area we were now walking was virtually treeless. These immense trees we were now seeing on this previously logged area made us aware of what nature can do for reforestation.

The path wound its way up following the contours of the land, making the climb to the back of the property much more manageable. We had been told that when we reached the most remote property line marker, our elevation would be about 400 feet higher than the river down at the other side of the property.

We sat and rested on an old tree stump, reflecting on what we had seen so far. After viewing and walking the fields on the lower side of the road, we had imagined that we could establish cross country ski trails winding around that wide expanse. The hilly and wooded terrain on this side of the road gave us a vision of a trail system following these hillside contours that would lead back to the house.

We filed those thoughts in our folder of dreams, and started our walk back down the hill on what would be the 400 foot elevation fall-line. As we emerged from the trees at the Town road that divided the property, we found ourselves now at the point of the car pull-off that we had stopped at the day before. If we followed from that point down to the bottom of the steep hill, we would find the rock face at the swimming hole. This was one of those times when our enthusiasm for this land led to trouble. I should more correctly say that my enthusiasm was the cause of this next episode.

We were at the road and could have easily walked along the road down the hill to the house and our car. But, there was still this hillside to explore. For readers of this story that are downhill skiers, this slope was equal to a Double Black Diamond ski slope loaded with trees. Actually, it probably was somewhat greater than that in difficulty. But, we weren't skiing and there were plenty of trees to hold as we made our way down. "Let's go!" I said with enthusiasm.

Sandra followed as we started down. It was difficult and we managed to negotiate by slowly doing what could be called basically a monkey walk, taking advantage of holding on to all the trees we could. In other words, we found ourselves frequently on hands and knees to keep from falling. I was in the lead and as I reached a point perhaps 15 to 20 feet above the steep rock face above the swimming hole, I started moving horizontally, and was able to reach a point beyond the rock face on a more moderate slope, where I could more easily climb down to the beach at the bottom.

Sandra, at that point, slipped, and began sliding down toward the rock face and the river. She desperately grasped for something to hold on to. As she was sliding, a piece of rock was dislodged and fell down onto her head. She managed to slide into a tree which stopped her before going over the rock face in to the river. With a supreme effort she was able to keep her senses and move horizontally where she could come down the rest of the way as I had done. The rock had cut her head and blood was flowing. I began to apply pressure, but without anything other than a handkerchief this was going to be a losing effort. Adding to our troubles, we were about one-half mile across the field from the house where our car was parked.

Fortunately, a family who lived across the river had been enjoying themselves in the swimming hole, and they saw what was happening. The water level was very low in the river above where the swimming channel began, so the man quickly waded across with a towel to apply pressure. I ran back to the house to get our car and drove back, past the barn through the field, and down as close to the swimming hole as possible. The family gave us driving directions to the hospital, as Sandra clearly required medical attention.

We made a fast trip, and fortunately the hospital was quiet on this Sunday afternoon so there was no wait for her to be seen by the emergency staff. We had a drive-by look at the hospital yesterday; this time it was up close and personal. From their excellent care which included stitches and a short rest, we got to know these kind caregivers.

Sandra was released and we started our drive home.

Do We Make an Offer?

We were back at home. Sandra's head was healing nicely. The stone she had dislodged in our down-the-hill episode had certainly cut her, but fortunately it was not as bad as it could have been. Her head was sore, of course, and it had bled profusely. The cut was about one-half inch long and was more of a penetration than a long gash. There hadn't been a need for shaving much of her hair, and the stitches could be covered by the combing of her hair. She was able to take it easy and use some of her relaxing time to think about the decision we should make.

I had to go back to work, but fortunately I was not scheduled for any travel that week so could take time to give some serious thought to this decision. The major decision for me would be changing from the corporate business life I had known with IBM over the last twenty-one years to that of owner of a very small business, not yet even established, and faced with many challenges.

First, I had to think of my IBM life history, and how much further that could take me. Over the first eleven years, I had been moved five times with job locations in Newark, New York City, White Plains, Raleigh, Washington, D.C. and finally Armonk, NY at the IBM Corporate Headquarters. During all of these assignments I had focused on IBM United States business, but with the Corporate position I also began working with IBM European based business.

This had led to a transfer and assignment to Paris, with a promotion to an executive management position. My product was a new Europe-Only communications product, engineered in France, and sold and serviced across six countries. This became a high pressure position with heavy attention from senior IBM corporate management. After finishing my three year assignment in Paris, I had moved back to White Plains, NY which was the U.S. based headquarters of the IBM

World Trade Corporation. My responsibility was product management for a broad base of products in the European marketplace. This involved travel to IBM engineering development laboratories largely within the U.S., and frequent travel back to Paris and other countries.

It was with this history, that this possibility of a new life had to be weighed. I was at an organization and salary level that would make promotional opportunities still quite possible but perhaps less frequent. The chances of another overseas assignment were probably at the fifty percent level. This was 1982 and I was fifty-three with another twelve years before normal retirement age. Did I want more of the same?

Having gone through the thought process, I could not see that staying with IBM would necessarily be our best decision. I examined myself and concluded I could be reaching an IBM burnout stage.

There was no question. We had fallen in love! The entire ambience of this Vermont property had totally thrilled us. But, could we leave the life we knew? Did we want to meet the challenges of this new way of life? There were several questions that had to be answered. Some of them were purely emotional and personal while others were objective and analytical.

Would a Country Inn produce enough business to support us? There was no real quantifiable way I could see to answer this question.

If the Inn business was not sufficient to support us, would the real estate value of the entire property give us enough return on a resale to justify the decision? The beauty and the size of the 115 acres would certainly support subdivision. When we made all the improvements in the house, the market value would, unquestionably be significantly increased.

Do we have enough financial resources to accomplish all the renovations/improvements we would like to make in the property? My estimates made me comfortable that we could meet our plan for changes.

These questions were major and of course they had subsets. And there would be other questions and unknowns that would develop. The single most important point to us was that of believing in ourselves.

We knew we could not take on such an adventure without total commitment.

Our intention would be to operate as a full inn; that is, to provide both breakfast and dinner. In our experience of staying at Inns, our most enjoyable times had been at those with full service.

Sandra had developed into an excellent cook and could handle the cooking. During our time of living in France, she had one-on-one training with an excellent chef and she planned to take more lessons at a known cooking school. Part of our recent discussions had been the changes we would make to upgrade the kitchen.

Our biggest issue was how to bridge the two-year gap between now and the planned date of early retirement. We needed to keep the working income coming in to finance all the renovations/improvements we felt necessary before opening for business. Unlike many such businesses that already operated as B&B's or Inns when owners changed hands, this would be an entirely new business, and we would have to build our reputation. It needed extensive renovation and it needed tender care to meet its potential.

This large property was being offered by the owners at a rather attractive price. We believed we could offer an even lower price that was nearly the same as we thought we could get for our Connecticut condominium home. Homes similar to ours had sold recently, and we felt confident the interior improvements we had made would help move it quickly.

We made the decision to change our life, and made an offer. Our thought process went like this; we will offer a reduced price, and if accepted we will sell our condominium. We will move into the farm house and begin the renovations. Sandra will live there full time, and I will take a rental apartment in Connecticut near my employer and commute to Vermont on weekends. This will be a two-year operation over which time the major work of renovation will be contracted out. Sandra will be there for the task of managing the work efforts and I will be there on weekends and vacations.

You can see this could be fraught with personal relationship dangers.

In actual fact, when we made the offer, the owners made a very reasonable counter-offer. We accepted and became the pending owners of a Vermont property of 115 acres plus house and four outbuildings.

Our life was going to dramatically change. We were going to trade a well-established and experienced life for one of change, uncertainty and probability of surprises.

Shortly after the formality of signing the contract, the owners invited us to stay with them for an overnight on the Columbus Weekend. We were thrilled and had a delightful time meeting them, and some of their friends who also had second homes in the area. It was an opportunity of learning more history about the home and the area, and to observe the love they had for this property.

Back in Connecticut, we placed our home on the market and fortunately our optimistic outlook held true. We essentially just traded mortgages even up. With the initial financial challenge out of the way, we were free to plan the closing on both ends as well as the movers for December 1st.

We were now definitely into it.

Moving and Settling In

Those next three months were a busy period. Our offer was negotiated, accepted, bank arrangements made, and the contract closed very quickly. One of the advantages of small town living is everything can be accomplished with a minimum of red tape. It was not as though we were operating on a hand shake basis, but it was very close to it with the recognition that details can be worked out.

For example, after the sales contract was agreed to and signed, we took another visit to look over the property and begin our detailed planning. We quickly saw a developing problem with the barn. As described, the barn had a high gambrel roof, and from the time we had first seen the structure to this visit, we now saw that the top of the front wall of the barn was beginning to tip out. The main beam attaching the front wall to the roof was separating, causing the wall to bow out. There was a real danger of the weight of the tall roof causing the front wall to collapse.

For us, the Buyers, it was natural that since we had not yet closed on the property, the responsibility to fix the barn would be with the Seller. The sellers said "this was an "*As Is"* contract and any repairs were our responsibility." Rather than get hung up in negotiations and see the barn continue getting worse, we asked the Realtor for his suggestion. He checked the problem out with a local contractor who said he could fix it. After the "fix" was explained to us with its low cost estimate, we agreed it would be done at our expense. This became our introduction to the common sense solutions to problems that we would find the norm in this area.

To simplify the explanation of how they fixed what would have become a major problem, this is what they did. The problem had been the case of nails pulling loose from the old wall beams so that there was no longer enough support to hold the horizontal beams tight to the vertical wall. The solution was to use a length of steel cable bolted through the back wall. Another length of cable was bolted through the front wall. These two lengths of cable, enough to span the distance from front to back wall, were then connected through a heavy duty cable puller. This device permitted the tightening of the full cable length, taking the slack out, which gradually pulled the front wall to a perfectly upright position. This was a short repair job with a low cost of $600. The actual cost is shown here to illustrate how this common sense approach with an honest work effort was typical of what we would receive from the trades over the coming years of living in this area - *honest value for honest work.*

While this was going on with the coordination of our realtor, we were back in Connecticut. We were back to our normal life, but also making plans for movers and discussing the sale of our condo with real estate brokers. We were feeling very good about selling, as we had added some nice features when we originally moved in. We ended up deciding to try and sell on our own. This was new as our past inter-city moves had always been done under the auspices of my employer with policies that offset the cost of our real estate commissions. We did some local advertising and word-of-mouth, and were quickly rewarded with interest in viewing our home. In a very short time we had a couple who wanted to buy and move in on a schedule that fit our needs perfectly.

It may help to understand what may appear to some, our almost casual approach to moving. We both lived our growing-up years in Toledo, Ohio. Sandra was born there and I was born in Pocahontas, Iowa three years earlier but was moved to the Toledo area as a Toddler. Both of us went to area schools. My family moved frequently enough I went to six schools by the time I was in he sixth grade. We both went on to graduate from the University of Toledo. We were married after my tour in the Marine Corps and immediately after Sandra's university graduation. We began our moving career two months later, as dictated by my first employer, AT&T, beginning with Detroit.

There were work location moves following Detroit: Cleveland, OH; New York City, White Plains, NY. IBM brought in more work moves beginning with Newark, NJ, New York City, White Plains, Raleigh, NC; Washington, DC; Armonk, NY; Paris, France; and White Plains, NY. The required inter-city moves had all been paid for by either by AT&T or IBM.

This move would be to Williamsville, VT where our Inn was to be located. This move would be our sole responsibility. I have spelled this out as it leads to another of the ***Rules that are critical to anyone considering Inn Keeping.***

> ***It is probably somewhat more rare than not, to find or create an opportunity to begin an Inn or B&B in the location where you are now living. There are, of course, those that are currently living in a large home or can find a large home to buy. This is more true for a B&B than an Inn. The simple definitions we are using in this book consider an Inn as one that will provide meals beyond breakfast. This generally requires a larger and more equipped kitchen and greater lounging/reception area. You may also assume a greater number of guest rooms.***
>
> ***Recognize that you may have to uproot yourself in order to find the opportunity and move to an area that is new. With that, you have to face what is a new life in a new location at the same time as beginning a new career. This is quite achievable, but if you have been comfortable living in the same home for some time the personal challenges may be difficult. Try to understand yourself and how you react to totally new things as you are making a decision on the business of inn keeping.***

The packing for our move was accomplished rather easily. Our experience from the many prior moves helped a great deal. The movers came and loaded the truck in the afternoon so they could begin the drive the next morning. While they were loading, we finished closing on the sale of the condo. We then drove to Vermont that evening so we could be at the closing for the Inn property in the morning. This closing was very smooth as we transferred ownership, and drove to our new house to await the arrival of the van.

During our last month in the condo, we had been busy taking advantage of living in the major New York metropolitan area with its greater shopping advantages. We knew that if we waited until we were living in the rural Vermont area, our access to shopping for the guest room furnishing and accessories we needed would be reduced. We had hustled around buying box springs, mattresses, pillows, bed linens and bathroom towels and arranging shipment to our condo so they could travel by the moving van. This was a wise decision as we could take advantage of volume discounts and sales prices. We had done enough room planning so that we could buy the right mix of king, queen, double and twin bed sizes. We knew it would be some long time before we could put them all to use, but what better place to store them?

The truck was unloaded and everything was moved in and placed for the time being. Boxes were unpacked to the extent we wanted at the time; paper work was signed, movers were tipped and the truck pulled out. We laid a fire in the fireplace in the living room, opened a bottle of wine and prepared to spend our first evening in our new home. Our condo living room furniture was a nice fit and we relaxed in front of the large living room fireplace.

The firewood blazing away and mesmerizing us was the result of one of the highly ethical workers I told you about earlier. Back shortly after we had signed the contract to buy, we had inquired of Dave for the name of someone to lay in firewood for us. I then talked with Brent who agreed to sell the wood at a price I understood to be $85.00 per cord. Since we would be going back to Connecticut, he would deliver it to our future Inn. In about two weeks we heard the wood had been delivered so I mailed him a check. About a week later, I received a telephone call at our condo from Brent, who told me I had made a mistake and sent him too much money. He explained the price was $80.00 and he would be returning the extra $5.00. I point this out because over the next several years he showed the same high level of business ethics typical for the majority of workers in this area.

The community we would be living next to was the small village of Williamsville, one-half mile down the road from us. The village center was a short, straight stretch of two lane road running along the upper bank of the Rock River. At the far end of this piece of road was a covered bridge; at the far end of the bridge the road went around a curve as it headed on west to another small village, and on to ski slopes.

The village center, in its early history, was an eighteenth century mill town located on the river with its picturesque dam. Now, for the most part, the remaining homes were residences for workers around the area as well as business' operating out of the homes. There was also a small church, a general store with a gas pump across the road, and a post office operating out of one of the homes. There were two side roads jutting off the side of the central road that ran up the hillside for some miles, through the wooded area, that had homes providing for the small population of the overall community.

Checking out the nearby areas was important to us. We headed out through the village and across the covered bridge so that we would be thoroughly familiar with the downhill ski areas. Since we were in early December we knew it wouldn't be long before we could see ourselves strapping on our skis to take advantage of one of our goals when we moved into this life. We were about 30 minutes from the first major ski area, Mt. Snow and 45 minutes from Stratton Mountain, so we found ourselves anticipating the pleasures we would be having. It is true that some years later we were finally able to take advantage of the skiing, but this leads to another important consideration in the decision.

> ***Inn keeping is a very busy life and if pleasure activities are most important to you, you might want to carefully consider what you are taking on. Time off from the Inn for personal reasons becomes a rare occurrence.***

After we had thoroughly checked out the ski areas, we then headed back past our Inn toward the closest main town, about eleven miles away, to check out the shopping scene. Remember, we had done that on our initial look, but this needed to be far more detailed. We spent some time visiting stores in Brattleboro and were pleased with the selection: traditional super market as well as a farmers market and health food store. There were also specialty stores, two of which became very helpful to us. The bakery was very good and had delicious baguettes which were very good for our French Toast recipe. The sea food store was special; the owners of the store made their daily trip to the Boston area so whenever we had seafood on the menu, it was fresh

We were feeling better and better about our decision.

The First Months

The first month was a whirlwind of activity. You might imagine what it is like if you have moved to a new home, into a new life to try out something you have never done before.

> ***This is the time to state another rule, one that either needs no stating or is so obvious that it could be left out. But, it must be said – if you are terrified by new things, think long and hard about your decision. If it is at all possible, try to time your beginning in the best weather in your clime. In our case, Winter in Vermont was always harsh. Stated simply, it could be very cold, windy, and snowy.***

None the less, we were so excited to begin this life that we threw ourselves into it with exuberance. The first week of December, I had taken the week off from work in New York, and between the two of us we were able to accomplish a majority of the unpacking and settling in the big house. We had invited a number of good friends to come stay with us over the week between Christmas and New Year. After all, we had all those mattresses and bedding we had gone shopping for prior to our move. Not only would it be fun, they would help us with some of the work projects, and we could celebrate the New Year in our new home.

I then had to go back to check in at work, and also make some arrangements for living during the work week. Our plan was for me to continue working in White Plains, New York and commute to and from Vermont on weekends. This would be a three-hour commute Monday mornings and Friday evenings. Sandra would be in Vermont and manage the ongoing projects during the week. I was lucky to very quickly find a basement apartment in Westport, Connecticut that was a daily commute quite similar to the one I had while living in our condo. This was going to be a tough life for both of us, but seemingly workable; in retrospect it was far more difficult for Sandra.

Most unfortunately, as I was arriving back at our Inn from this first week commuting trip, Sandra received a telephone call that her Mother had gone in the hospital and was in serious condition. Sandra quickly made plans for us to fly to Toledo where the rest of the family lived. After a few short days we decided I would go back to Vermont to be there for all the committed guests, and Sandra would stay with her Mother until she passed on. She and our son, Jon, were able to be there for her funeral. It was a sad time, but unfortunately commitments to guests in the hospitality business often interfere with personal needs. It was a very trying time for Sandra, and she returned to Vermont just after the first of the year.

Our personal friends did arrive in the week between Christmas and the New Year. Of course, they were very sad for Sandra and disappointed she wasn't there, but all dug in and worked on the various tasks that had been planned out. The men, fortunately, were all very handy types and accomplished several tasks ranging from construction repair to running speaker wire connecting high-fidelity components. It would be great to have these guys around all the time.

The women proved to be very valuable as they took over doing much of the box unpacking that Sandra had not been able to finish in the time between the move and the sudden trip to Toledo. Their storage locations turned out to be right on the money as Sandra discovered after she returned. On New Year's Day we all took a break and went up on the upper meadow for a picnic in the snow – fortunately, it was a bright, sunshine day and made the last day for all these friends most memorable.

Heavy snows had begun late that winter, just before we had made the trip to Toledo. And the falling snow continued with intensity, so that by the first of February we had a full seven feet of accumulated snow on the ground. Contrary to what some will think, this is a beautiful sight. First of all, Vermont is equipped to handle snow; the roads are generally kept well plowed by Town road crews. Homes usually have an arrangement with a local resident with a truck and snow plow to keep their driveways clear. There are always exceptions of course, but I am speaking of the majority who keep their paths cleared. Snow blowers are a common sight, and we quickly added one to our equipment list with me as the operator.

The beautiful sight I am referring to is the woodland. The undergrowth that is found in most woodland areas has been covered by deep snow. You can look across and through the trees and see nothing but virgin snow. And then you strap on a set of snowshoes and take off through the woods walking across the top of all the snow, unencumbered by any brush. This is truly an exhilarating experience. The newer, high tech snowshoes are lighter and fully support your weight. If you can't ski, either down-hill or cross-country, this is the next best thing to heaven in the snow.

It was, of course, not all fun as we did have a number of must-do things. One of the first things we learned was that the antiquated heating system was not going to be satisfactory. We had realized there were two systems. The main part of the house had a large oil furnace that had been installed nearly forty years earlier, and was not only very large but very inefficient. Adding to that was the fact we were at a time of burgeoning oil prices. The back part of the house had been wired for electric heat which was even more expensive than oil. When we received our first bills, it didn't take long to have a recommended heating engineer come out and consult. We made our decision on the replacement system, but would have to wait until mild weather for the actual installation.

In our second month, we had a rather major situation develop that shows the range of problems you can have with old homes in the north-country. Jon had asked us if we could possibly accept having a large number of his post-college age friends come up for a long weekend of skiing. There was no way we would actually be ready for paying Inn guests, but as long as they knew it would be a high level of roughing it without costing them anything, they were well pleased.

Just before the large group was to arrive, we had some other guests stay with us. These were very dear friends that we had known for years. Our relationship went back to pre-kindergarten days for Sandra and the mother, Donna, and going back to college days for me and Emil. They had come up for some skiing with their children and had thoroughly enjoyed themselves. We had not joined them for the skiing on this trip as there was just too much for us to do in beginning our Inn life. They had packed up their car in the morning to go back home to

Connecticut, and we said our goodbyes. As they were pulling out of the driveway, Sandra came out of the house and while waving to our friends, quietly said to me, "Bill, we have a problem; our septic tank has backed up and it is coming out of our washing machine in the basement."

Needless to say, this was an exciting moment to occur at any time, but with the prospect of a large group coming to stay the next day it was sheer dread. Fortunately, Jon, our son, had already arrived in anticipation of the next day's group, and he had the wits to be able to find a way to quickly plug the septic line to cut off the back-up flow. *To you as a reader this may not be a pleasant story to read, but it was in fact a real, and serious, situation – and one of the purposes of this book is to let you know this* ***Rule:***

***Expect the unexpected*.**

We were most fortunate that the former owners had written their useful telephone numbers on the moulding of the window next to the wall telephone. Luckily, *Amon, Plumber*, along with his number, was prominent on the list. As I was concentrating my efforts in the basement with Jon, Sandra called the Plumber. He was home and understood the situation immediately. He said he would be out and did we have a backhoe? The answer to that was, No!

He arrived, followed by the backhoe and its operator, and diagnosed the problem. They proceeded to dig a temporary leach pit with a new line from the septic tank to the leach pit. Amon explained: the original line from the tank had been dug down the center of the road in front of the house, and across to a leach pit on the other side of the road. This had been dug some years prior to the black top that now paved the road. Every winter, the ground freezes, and the freezing depth is made even deeper under the roads due to the car traffic driving the frost line deeper. It is not unusual in Vermont for the frost line to be at least four feet deep; thus, the frozen sewer line and our problem. After the winter had passed we completed a replacement system which you will read about in a later chapter.

This was the first of several occasions to use the valuable services of our Plumber, and each time Amon rose to the occasion.

Beginning the Inn Renovation

We had made it through the first two months of a very active moving-in time and were now in a position to begin the renovation that would eventually turn this house into The Country Inn at Williamsville. We had discussed some of the many changes we would have to make and had made a partial list. We avoided listing everything, as a complete list could become frightening – it seemed better to take the listing slowly so that we could more easily see progress. One of the advantages of my weekly commutes was that it gave the chance to mentally plan the projects while I was driving. I could then work on them over the weekends.

As might be expected, it became obvious that there were many projects ahead that required technical skills I did not have. It was now highly unlikely the renovation could be finished and open for business in the desired two-year time frame, when I could take an early retirement. This realization did not dampen our spirits and interest, but it did bring to bear the fact we would definitely need more help.

Rather than trying to do everything ourselves, it became obvious we should take on the role of General Contractor and begin lining up the Carpenters, Electricians, Plumbers, Heating, Flooring, Roofing, Wallpapering, and Painting (Interior as well as Exterior). I had skills in planning, drawing of plans, and some basic building skills, so it would work well for me to handle the basic design and planning the work schedule. Sandra, with her training in the culinary arts would handle the kitchen requirements as well as laundry and bath plans. We needed local knowledge to line up the subcontractors.

We had some nearby neighbors that, early on, had dropped by our home to welcome us to Vermont. They were both artists living in a delightful home nestled on the river bluff about one-half mile from our Inn. They had extended an invitation to us for Brunch along with another couple. Of the other couple, the husband was an attorney and his wife, while cosmopolitan, operated their large property as a local farmer. We all got along very well, and the lawyer over time represented us in all of our legal involvements. In brunch conversation, these new friends offered us many very helpful ideas on local tradespeople we could use in our project.

The attorney then brought up something that would become a major regulatory factor in our ability to follow through with our dream. He referred to VERMONT ACT 250 as a requirement in the State Approval Process for our Inn. This was a shock as no-where in our review of the property, had there been any mention of regulations on use of the property as a country inn. This is not being written as a complaint, as we were finally able to work through the process and open the Inn. ACT 250 did add considerable work effort for me in preparing the required documentation for review by State authorities. It did involve the hiring of legal support, the hosting of on-site reviews by State bodies, and meetings before the local Town Board.

The Vermont Act 250 is, simply, a development control Act designed by the State to complicate, in our eyes, all small business owners and innkeepers attempting to establish simple businesses in Vermont. The steps in the review and approval process for a small business such as this are the same as though the business seeking approval was, perhaps, a large manufacturing facility or a large retailer.

And not only just for our Inn; as long as a business or development of any kind is approved under Act 250, the same approval process would then be required for any further development we attempt for any additional land we own in the area. For example, you will read later in this book that we sold the Inn property, and wished to build our own personal home on a retained subdivided portion of our total property. This review and approval process for our new home involved the same burdensome and costly requirements as we had gone through for the original commercial Inn. The same criteria also applied for the other subdivisions of land we performed late in our ownership.

All of this does clearly establish the significance of this **Rule**:

Pay particular attention to all rules and regulations, Local, State and Federal that will apply to the business you intend to operate. This will apply not only to an existing hospitality industry business, but to any rules or regulations that may be required if you are converting from one zoning classification to another.

This is a responsibility you must assume. You cannot assume that a real estate broker will bring all pertinent regulations to your attention, without specifically requesting the information and/or advice for your consideration. You must ask. Before signing a purchase contract, ask your attorney to review this for all applicable Laws, Regulations and/or Permits that will apply.

The friends we had met at the Brunch had given us good leads on lining up the key workers that would become so critical to us. The most important to us in the near term were Carpenter, Electrician and Plumber. Our plumber was Amon DeWitt, the electrician was Gene Garbe, and the carpenter was Bill Cobb. Originally, we had thought we could use the carpenter who had handled the barn repair, but it turned out that was his last job before retiring from carpentry and opening up his own landscaping nursery business. Fortunately, his senior carpenter, Bill, was now on his own and going to be available so he could take on projects for us. I could lay out the various projects these men could work on, and with me gone during the week Sandra could oversee their efforts and communicate with me by telephone as necessary.

There was one other man who became vital to us. Ed Druke was a lifelong resident of Williamsville and lived with his family near the top of the hill that rose above our Inn property. We had met Ed shortly after we had contracted to buy, but before closing. We had driven up from our condo on one of our get acquainted trips, and as we were looking around the home and barn, Ed pulled into the driveway in the red pick-up truck we would always associate with good feelings. It would be a rare occasion when he wouldn't have his tape deck playing classical orchestra music. He introduced himself and let us know he had served as a caretaker for the current owners, since they no longer spent much time using their property. We would get to know Ed and his family quite well.

Now that we had the introduction to Act 250, we decided we should definitely have an attorney to help guide us through the Vermont State procedures and it made sense to work with Fred Houston, whom we had met at the neighbor's brunch. He put us in touch with the Vermont Office that could provide us with the appropriate rules and regulations. We then realized what the major criteria were that would guide us through the approval adventure. Now that we knew who would be our principal subcontractors working with us, we began contacting the major State functions that would have a voice in the final approval of our Inn. This brings up another **Rule:**:

> ***Since your project will eventually require specific final approvals, such as Health Inspection, Fire Inspection, etc., invite the involved State, Local, or even Federal key personnel to meet you at your project early on in the project. You will gain immeasurably from this effort, both in the personal touch of meeting them as well as gaining an understanding of any particular requirements they are sensitive to.***

We found these visits especially helpful in our pre-planning phase and were able to include several changes in our designs and construction that smoothed our final approvals.

The first major effort was to set up a project list for Bill, the carpenter, to begin work. The existing design of the house consisted of three sections; the original building from the late 1700's, the major section that was added circa 1830, and the third section in the 1960's which was the closing-in of the carriage house and attaching it to the back of the original building to form the "L".

The ground floor of the original building included a room that served as the kitchen, opening with a door to the dining room in the major section. The kitchen had a door with two steps out to a front walkway, and a door out the back that led into what had been the carriage house. There was also a stairway up to two bedrooms and a bathroom on the second floor, and a stairway down to the basement. Also on the ground floor there was a storage room as well as a room that could be converted to a laundry.

The carriage house had been remodeled as a recreation room plus storage rooms with a spiral staircase that led upstairs to dormitory-like rooms. The new design would convert the recreation room to a larger commercial kitchen for Sandra to display her skills. The existing kitchen would be converted to a second dining room.

There would be much more to come, but for now our carpenter could begin his work.

Continuing Renovation

While I was away at my job in White Plains, New York the work effort continued in Vermont. Sandra would make notes on any questions our carpenter would have during the day, and in the evening she would discuss with me by telephone. She would pass on the decisions we had reached when Bill came in the next day. This was all working very well, and when I would drive up on Friday evenings I was always impressed with how well the renovation effort was proceeding.

However, not everything was anticipated. One time when I arrived at the end of the week, Sandra greeted me with a smile and "Bill, the door to our powder room won't close." A trip to the basement found the problem. One of the ceiling beams had broken due to a long-time-ago powder post beetle infestation that had not been corrected, when the rest of beams had been replaced. Our carpenter, Bill, took care of the beam replacement problem and with the corrected balance the door resumed proper operation. We were going to find other problems were going to pop-up, but all of them were fixable.

Meanwhile, the renovation effort was moving along. We found that once the current linoleum kitchen floor covering was removed that we had a lovely birds-eye maple floor underneath. Proper sanding and refinishing resulted in a spectacular floor in what would become the new second dining room. While this was going on, arrangements were being made to set up a temporary kitchen in the former recreation room. This required a temporary sink and stove arrangement until the extensive work could be completed for the new professional kitchen.

When the former owner had closed in the carriage house for use as a recreation room, they had not included a plan for providing running water and sewer facilities to that addition. As a result, they had needed just enough clearance between the floor joists and existing ground level so that the new floor was the same height as the floors in the rest of the house. Thus, in order to provide water and sink drainage lines for the new kitchen, we had to take up the recreation room floor and dig trenches for running the water and drain lines. Amon, our plumber, provided the guidance on this effort and I, along with a local teenager, dug the trenches. Amon then ran the drain and water lines for our new kitchen. Next, our carpenter built the floor joists and laid the new flooring, so we could install the temporary sink and stove for use during the remodeling.

Work on the new second dining room continued. The old kitchen had a single window over the sink that had been installed on the back wall. This sink and window were removed, and in their place a double door with full glass and mullions was installed. That now offered a view out the back of the house that was further enhanced with the building of an outside deck that crossed over most of the back of the house.

The front wall of this former kitchen had been a window and an outside door with the two steps down to the front walkway. The door and window were removed and replaced with a full double-width window with mullions matching the door on the other wall. We now had a view looking out across the fields and hills beyond. The front door that we replaced was now moved into another room, and was used as the door out to a new front porch. One of the interesting aspects of this change is that this door ended up exactly where a door had been in this house's previous life. Also interesting, when we subsequently added an outside door in the living room, we also found there had been a door in a previous life.

All of these changes may be difficult to follow, but we have now, essentially, remade the living style of the house.

When the Fire Inspector had been out to visit us, he had insisted on having a fire escape stairway installed on the exterior. The house had such clean lines that on our first reaction, it didn't seem right to add stairs to its outside lines. On study of a past picture of the house from approximately 1900, we saw there may be a way. There had been a porch across the front of the house that had been removed at some time. From the old photograph, the porch appeared to be about four feet deep, but it occurred to us that if we made a new porch deep enough to match the eight foot setback of the "L" it would give a harmonious look. This would then allow us to extend the new porch beyond the house the width of a stairway in such a way as to mask the appearance of the fire escape so that it would appear to have been built with the house. This met the Fire Inspector's need, and it was interesting – shortly after the porch had been constructed, one of the local village residents insisted the porch was not new, that it had been there all along.

Other carpentry changes involving the exterior focused on the back of the house. We had determined we would use the back as the prime entrance for guests. The house was rather close to the road, and our parking area was going to be better situated toward the rear. Another requirement levied on us through the Act 250 Hearing Process was energy related. The primary entrance door had to be equipped with an air-lock. This means that there must be an air space between two doors so that guests could step inside the air space and close the outside door before opening the actual inside entrance door. This, of course, was intended to prevent the loss of heated air.

Our solution to this was to build an entrance room on the back of the house so that guests would be completely in the air-lock room before entering the house. This would allow guests to enter into the gracious living room. During the winter the windows for this air-lock room would be storm windows, and during mild weather they would be removed and replaced with screens. This design was harmonious with the overall design of the home, and permitted the deck to be constructed across the back wall of the two dining rooms. The double door on the second dining room wall opened on this deck. The large window that was part of the primary dining room was then converted into a triple door also opening on the new deck. The overall design with front porch and back deck now permitted easy indoor and outdoor flow providing social movement for guests and enjoyment of the nature surrounding the Inn. The deck became a perfect addition for guest flow during events such as wedding receptions.

That generally describes the construction work that was underway on the first floor. The second floor would also be in for its share. When we originally purchased, there were a total of ten bedrooms and three bathrooms on the second floor. Our objective was to have all guest rooms with a private bathroom, plus our owner's suite with its bathroom. By eliminating three of the dormitory type rooms, and some judicial design and construction work, we would finish with six guest rooms with their private baths.

Some Unusual Experiences

This is the chapter where I group some of the unusual experiences that must be told to give "full flavor" to our adventure of preparing the Inn.

You will recall our earlier experience of trouble with our septic system, and that it was repaired on a temporary basis. We, of course, followed all the proper procedures in contracting with an engineer who would design our new system. We had examined our possibilities for a new septic system layout on the side lawn near the house on a natural level area. There was very little level land near the house, and as we looked at our side yard this had seemed a perfect location for our new system.

Our engineer came out to dig some test pits to determine if the ground where the septic field was planned was going to be satisfactory. It was definitely not workable. There were indications of underground springs being active, and the soils were too wet for satisfactory percolation. This was indeed disappointing, but as we were learning, there is nothing that can't be fixed. It is basically a function of having the right professionals involved, and the money to pay for it.

Our engineer then designed a state-of-the-art "mound system" with a large septic tank near the house connected to a large overflow tank at the bottom of the hill behind the house. This was connected to another tank half-way up the hill. A line then ran up from that tank up to septic fields designed in the mound system that was located in soils giving proper distribution of the effluent. Since this was to be a commercial business, the system was designed with dual pumps in each tank that alternated operation and insured back-up. These tanks were equipped with high-level alarms to alert us, should anything go wrong.

This gives rise to another **Rule**:

> ***Be prepared for anything, keep your wits about you and look for common sense solutions.***

We are going to jump ahead to a winter experience that occurred after we had opened the Inn and were operating with a full house of guests.

> *The time was President's Weekend in February in the dead of winter with its snows and cold. There are three periods when you expect to be the busiest of the year – and are always fully booked; these are Fall Foliage, New Year Weekend and President's Weekend. The weekend had started and the alarm went-off signaling a problem. This was the first time in the four years since installation of our system that an alarm had sounded – AND WE HAD A FULL HOUSE.*
>
> *The first thing I did was check the levels in the overflow tanks. They were full which is not supposed to happen with the pump system. We placed a call to the engineer, but found he was out in Colorado on the ski slopes and would call back. Next, we called the septic tank company who usually provided the routine pumping maintenance. They would come out to pump the tanks, and fortunately their truck was just large enough to take the full septic system contents.*
>
> *With a full house of guests it was going to fill up again which meant nearly a full time job for the driver unless we could fix the problem. Vermont is not a big state and does not have very large sanitary dumping facilities. We found that each time they pumped, they would have to drive across the bottom of the state and over a mountain range from Brattleboro to Bennington in order to dump.*
>
> *When the engineer came off the Colorado ski slope, he picked up his message and called. He suggested a solution that required finding the center point of the snow-covered septic fields at the top of the hill. This was a* daylight job

so we had to put off any action until morning. We did call Amon, our plumber, and arranged for him to be with us in the morning. The assumption was a frozen pipe problem up on the hill, and I then confirmed there was ice in the force field line. Amon had our son-in-law, Darren, carry a bucket of hot water up the hill where he poured that on the dead center of the pipe at the center of the designed force field. That quickly thawed the frozen spot, and saved the weekend. It seems that the system design, which followed the design spec of the state, had a design flaw. We easily corrected that by drilling a small drainage hole in a pipe in the tank and never had another problem.

We had two other unusual experiences that involved Amon. Both of these occurred during the first year in our renovation when I was actively commuting.

We had a dog whose name was Gayla. We didn't know her very well as we had just taken her from friends who could no longer care for their dog with their new-infant-in-the-family situation. I arrived home on a late Friday evening and learned from Sandra that Gayla had just refused to drink the water from her dish. This was strange, as the experience I had with dogs was they would seem to drink most anything. Whenever any aspect of our house renovation involved water we would call Amon, so he stopped by on Saturday morning.

After listening to our description of the situation he said, "you might have a furry critter in your spring house."

He went on to explain what we should do to disinfect our water system if that was the problem. Our water system was rather ingenious. It started about six-hundred feet up the hill behind the house. There were two separate springs providing fresh clear water; each spring was covered with a small building protecting the water source from the elements. These were connected by one-half inch pipes running down the hill about one-hundred feet where they connected with a "Y" into a single pipe that ran five-

hundred feet down to the house basement. The basement had a cistern that would hold about seventeen hundred gallons of water, constantly refreshed with the spring water. You would have to have water as fresh and clear as this to know just how good it was; untouched by any artificial chemicals, it was as close to perfect as possible.

Amon suggested some small animal may have burrowed its way under one of the spring houses and had died in the water, so we would have to disinfect. This would require buying two gallons of bleach and pouring one in the spring house and one in the cistern. We could let the bleach do its job of disinfecting over the next week while I was away, then I could clean the spring house when I returned the next weekend. Sandra would do the job of cleaning the cistern in the house at that time. We were fortunate in having a separate well as a back-up for the spring water, so we had water while this process was underway.

After Amon explained this process to us, he left it to us to carry on the investigation of the spring house and to begin the disinfecting. As he was leaving, he paused at the door, turned, gave us a little smile, and asked in good humor,

"have you had any hair come out of your faucet yet?

Sure enough, I went up the hill, opened the door in one of the spring houses, looked down at the water level and saw: a bloated woodchuck floating belly-up with a small bare patch of skin showing. We followed through with the cleaning process Amon had directed, and life went on as the cistern began filling to normal.

However, our water story didn't end there. We found that our back-up well wasn't going to be adequate for our commercial venture. We had always known that the Health Department wouldn't let us operate an Inn with natural spring water, but we had assumed our well would be sufficient. Shortly after our woodchuck experience, we found the well was too shallow and had run dry.

We thought: no big problem now, as we had our spring water and full cistern, but we should begin drilling a new well. Naturally, we called on Amon to manage the process for us, and after consulting on the location for the well, I told him where we wanted it to be drilled, close to the house. The big drilling rig was brought in on Monday, drilling was begun, and I returned to my commuting.

> *The following weekend, Sandra and I awakened on Saturday morning, turned on a faucet and no water! Down to the basement to investigate, and the cistern was empty. Up to the spring houses, open the doors; water was overflowing across the ground, but still no water coming into the cistern. The drilling rig was still there as they hadn't finished their job. After more detective work, we found the problem. The giant drilling rig had been placed where I had told him, which unknown to me or Amon, was precisely over the underground location of the water line that ran from the spring houses down to our house. That one-half inch pipe had been pinched off by the big drilling bit, and the flow of the water was blocked. It was rather like finding the needle in the haystack. It was a simple task to then splice in a section of flexible pipe around the blockage for water to begin its flow again. As soon as the new well was complete and began to function, we had a little celebration and retired the spring houses.*

Outdoor Activities

Trail System

One of the early outdoor initiatives we undertook, as the weather moved from the spring of our first year into the early days of summer, was the beginning preparation for the winter operation of our future Inn. We had started thinking of a cross-country ski operation for our Inn when we began walking the property during our first visits. During that recent first brunch we had with our neighbors, we discussed skiing and were told that George, one of the village residents, had experience that tied in nicely. He had been a cross-country ski coach, and was also by profession a forester, with experience in managing logging operations.

Later on, we invited George to stop by and told him of our interest in setting up a trail system. He was quite familiar with our property, and believed it had excellent features for cross-country. Our property had both moderate and relatively steep wooded terrain, as well as open flat fields, that would adapt well for setting out tracked cross-country skiing trails. He felt we could take advantage of the heavy woods by setting up a timbering program that would develop logging trails we could use later for skiing. A major benefit of this would be the income from sale of the timber. The major wood crop would be pine with some hard wood. As a forester, he would lay out the trails and trees to be cut, and would work with the loggers in supervision of the entire effort. As a result of George's selective marking, there would be no clear-cutting by the loggers.

This turned out to be an excellent decision, and resulted in a clean operation with little to no slash left on the ground, and a well-designed skiing trail system. We ended up with a desired open appearance throughout our wooded areas. The pines that were taken out were all large. The only prior logging, as we learned from local history, had been done 75 to 80 years ago. As an indicator of the size of the pines we had, the saw mill had a restriction on the diameter size they could take through their mill. This was a maximum of 28 inches, and a majority of the logs we had cut had to be carefully measured to ensure they were not too large for the saw mill.

George first walked the entire wooded areas and marked the trees to be cut and removed. In addition to the special attention given to being selective in the marking of trees it was also necessary to establish logging trails. These had to follow contours of the land for the movement of logging equipment to haul out the cut timber. These trails would then be used to set up the cross-country ski trails.

George managed the bidding for loggers, the selection of the winning bid, and overseeing the entire logging operation. When it was all finished, we had an operation that resulted in approximately 300,000 board feet of pine and 100,000 of hard wood from the land on both sides of the road. This operation provided some prime timber and a decent financial outcome. An additional benefit of this careful marking and supervision was the logging completion without harm to the overall woodland effect.

Even though the trails had been initially established by the logging operation, there was still effort required. These trails were intended for winter skiing, but they also had to serve for hiking in other times of the year. This meant building and grooming. There were occasional small streams running through the woods, and down the hillside, that would have to have bridges built, low hanging limbs pruned, rocks moved, and other general light maintenance. These tasks fell to me to do and complete the required ongoing maintenance.

There was one fortunately little episode while working on the trail building. I was being helped by a nearby neighbor, Bud Randall, who fortunately really had his wits about him. I had my tractor up on the hill with us, making use of the front loader to move some rocks. I had made the mistake of maneuvering the tractor into a position on a side hill. I moved it again slightly, but just enough that my center of gravity was off. The tractor began to tip over downhill with me in the seat, and I could have ended up with the tractor on top of me. Bud saved the day. He alertly jumped on the lower rim of the tractor's large rear wheel on the up-hill side, and his weight provided just enough counter balance that it stopped the downhill tipping. I was able to once again maneuver the tractor to regain proper position and balance.

I am bringing this up because I was saved from potential injury, and it reminded me of a similar story involving the former owner and his tractor. I have told you of the farm equipment stored in the barn. I had observed that the tractor had an upward bend in the driver's foot support board, and inquired about it with Ed. I was told that the owner had been on his tractor working on the side hill of the steeper slope between the pond and the road. He had put himself in a position where he had exceeded the center of gravity and tipped over. He was thrown off downhill and hit the ground ending up just on the downhill side of a rock. The tractor followed him, and luckily, the tractor's foot support board hit that rock, and because of the spring steel in the support, bounced up enough to clear the owner as it bounced further down the hill. He avoided serious injury.

Jumping ahead several years, after opening the Inn, it also was my winter job to groom the cross-country trails at a minimum of each time it snowed. This task was done primarily with fresh and typically heavy snow, almost always early in the day, and cold. The primary machine used was a snowmobile. I had bought a special machine, built with a double wide track, that was heavy – 800 pounds. Fortunately, there was a good windshield that provided some protection for me, and it was designed so that the motor heat kept the hands warm. This was important as the skiing tracks for guests required several passes around the trails. Cumulatively, this involved several miles of towing different pieces of equipment each time I groomed the trails..

Since we had both hilly, wooded trails and flatter fields, the effort involved a variety of different experiences. There were many snowfalls over the course of the winter and each snowfall would add complexity. For example, once a trail was groomed, the snow packed down and became firm underneath. After the next snowfall, the track is easier to set. However, the next time is a challenge to track in the same trail. The freshly fallen snow covers existing tracks, and if you find yourself drifting off the trail, the snow underneath will be quite soft, and the snowmobile will sink into the deeper snow. It was not uncommon to have the snowmobile stuck in the soft snow. When that happened, this special design 800 pound snowmobile could be a bear to get back on track.

There were two solutions, both involving a shovel; it was normal to carry one of the big coal-type shovels on the snowmobile, so the digging could be done rather quickly to make it possible to drive the snowmobile up on the track. That was true on the open hay fields. The other solution could be used in the woods, where it was possible to use a combination of the shovel and a chain. I would hook the chain to the snowmobile and the other end to a tree. Then, using a device called a "come-along", it was possible to winch my way out.

Grooming snow trails could be a long, cold job, but it was always very satisfying, leaving me with a healthy, strong feeling of accomplishment, best enjoyed with the indoor warmth of a wood stove or fireplace. Reading all of this, you might wonder how frequently it snowed. I didn't keep a count except for our last winter, and that year it snowed sixteen times with each snowfall a minimum of six inches.

Haying

Another outside activity, that involved a great amount of time, was haying the fields. For some years Ed had an arrangement with the former owners whereby he would fertilize the fields. When the fields were ready for haying, he would bring his equipment, cut and bale the hay, manage the sales, and keep the proceeds. That was an arrangement good for the owners and for Ed. I had discussed with Ed that I would plan on taking over the haying when we took up full time living there, but meanwhile Ed could continue the haying arrangement.

When we began the full time Vermont life after retirement from England, I visited the farm equipment dealer and bought the necessary equipment. This was an overall expensive outlay of cash, but the equipment with proper maintenance could last for years. This involved a Farm Tractor and all of the specially designed haying equipment. This includes a side-mounted Cutter Bar for mowing, a Tedder for fluffing the cut hay lying on the field to enhance drying, a Hay-Rake to form rows of hay, and the Baler to create the bales of hay. Additionally, a Trailer to be pulled by the tractor was necessary to move the hay to the barn.

The other equipment required was a Hay Elevator to move the hay up to the barn loft. This last piece was essentially a type of electrically driven conveyor belt that would have one end on the trailer, and the other up through the door on the second floor of the barn. In addition to this haying equipment, I also bought a Back-Hoe and Front Loader that I could mount on the tractor for other jobs around the Inn and Farm. Oh yes, let's not forget the Pickup Truck.

Haying is essentially a two-day operation for each section of fields being processed. Our fields were a six-day operation to cover all sections. Up until the last phase of clearing the bales off the field, it is a one-person operation that is both mind-numbing and butt-numbing. The farmer is on the tractor going around and around in a series of clockwise turns from the outside-in until all the hay is cut. The cutter bar is then detached and stored, and the "tedder" is attached, and driving the same track begins again. This piece of equipment is pulled, causing a series of counter-rotating tines to fluff and scatter the freshly cut hay. This allows air to circulate while the cut hay is on the ground hastening the drying operation. The tedding follows the same direction as the mowing. Normally, the tedding is repeated so that two complete operations can be accomplished twice within this first day. This hay is then left on the field overnight.

The next morning, there will still be some moisture left in the hay due to the overnight dew. This morning cycle is the only time when there is much to think about while riding around the field; the freshly cut and tedded hay has attracted deer overnight. The thought process I am referring to is rather dull; that is, to wonder just how many deer have been on the field overnight. You can see their tracks everywhere throughout the field: they apparently liked the hay for nibbling.

One more round of tedding normally resulted in dry hay, and it was ready for raking into rows. Thorough drying of the hay is critical. If it is baled damp, it becomes musty and could over time become moldy. Horses eating damp hay will develop colic. They can die.

Depending on the number of workers, it may be possible to have some overlap on raking and baling. As the rows are being raked, the baler may begin following along with the baler doing its job of scooping up the hay, creating bales, tying and spitting out the bales. If the hay is being sold off the fields, the customers may be following with their trucks and gathering up the bales.

Those bales that have not been spoken for and picked up off the field will be loaded on the trailer and moved up to the barn where they will be placed on the electric elevator for storage in the hay loft. This latter part of the day is when the labor intensive phase begins and the volunteers who show up are indeed welcome. Volunteers are good-hearted neighbors and local residents who recognize how labor intensive this effort is, and come to jump into the work flow. It doesn't take long and the camaraderie seems to flow. When the work is all done, the beer and soda is taken off ice for a celebration and many a thank you is heard.

All of this explanation on haying assumes the weather is clear and dry. Cloudy, heavy or rainy days are terrible for hay farmers. Days that start out clear and turn rainy are worse than a full day of rain. If full, rainy days occur, the farmer will lose a day, but the hay hasn't been cut and will wait for the first good day. The days that start clear can turn into rain and ruination of hay for horses. Horses were the market for hay in our area. We did have some days when the hay was ruined and we had to look for someone to buy the bad bales. Fortunately, I found the downhill ski slopes could use bales, and road construction companies could help by using hay bales for erosion control. The old adage, ***Make hay while the sun shines*** is one of the most important parts of a hay farmer's life.

Since I was taking over our haying, Ed no longer had any responsibility nor had this hay as a source of income. But, being the responsible man he was, he recognized I knew nothing of this process and business. He stepped right in and taught me how to handle the entire process, and he directed his past customers to buy the hay from me. Also for the hay that was not being sold right off the fields, he helped line up volunteers to pick up hay bales from the field and load them into the barn. Ed would continue being a friend over the entire time we had the Inn.

Sandra's Culinary Skills

Dinners were to become the most important part of our Country Inn. Our location was a superior setting, the house was on its way to becoming a renovated country-side masterpiece. We as inn keepers were a personable and welcoming couple, and the Dinners would set it all off.

Sandra's culinary training began in France some years before our decision was reached to create the Country Inn. I don't believe there may have even been an inkling of an idea of her future. Her primary goal at the time was to expose herself to the grand cuisines of France. We had moved to Paris with our children for a three-year assignment with my Company. I became quickly and deeply involved in the European International Headquarters with specific responsibilities involving the countries of France, Germany, Italy, Belgium, Finland and England. The children were also quickly immersed in their schooling, and Sandra set about learning the French language. She also volunteered with the American Women's Group and served as Editor of the monthly newsletter for the American School.

It was with the Women's Group that Sandra learned of potential Culinary Programs. The one that most intrigued her and started her on the path, leading to her expertise and eventual chef's role at our Country Inn, was an individual one-on-one program with a remarkable teaching chef. The course this chef had perfected was a Classic Fish Course of five lessons. He would work only with Sandra in her home kitchen with her own implements one day per week for the five weeks. This required his journey from his home by the Paris Metro, and then by train from Paris to the suburb where we lived. He would then walk to our home and arrive by 9:00 a.m. Prior to his arrival at our home, he would have advised Sandra what ingredients she should have for them to work with. Early in the morning she would go to the open market to buy the fresh market ingredients, just as all the Paris restaurant chefs would be doing for their daily menus. Just this aspect by itself would start her day with high anticipation.

The Chef was John Desmond who was from Southern Ireland. He had attended Hotel School in Ireland and began working in restaurant management in Berlin at the Hotel Bristol Kempinski. He moved from there to Paris to train in the kitchens of the famous Ritz Hotel. After a year he went to the Paris three star restaurant "Taillevent" where he gained further experience in Sauce, Fish and Pastry. He joined the staff of "La Varenne" Cooking School as one of their teaching chefs.

During this time in Paris he branched out into private teaching which is when Sandra made her contact with him. His long term goals involved writing cook-books, then touring as a guest lecturer to be followed by his return to Ireland to open an exclusive restaurant; all of which he accomplished. He was outstanding as a teaching chef, and Sandra learned a great deal as well as making a good friend.

For his program with Sandra, he would spend the morning with her, preparing a full luncheon, after which he would give her the menu and ingredients needed for the lesson the following week. Upon his departure, Sandra's guests would arrive for a wonderful 1:00 p.m. luncheon. At the conclusion of the five-week course Sandra had developed a series of fine menus that she used to produce memorable dining experiences for our friends over the coming years. John also catered two fine dinners personally for us, and our dinner guests, prior to our final departure from France.

We had the occasion to see him again some years later as he was touring the U.S. with a colleague on a combination catering and guest lecture tour. Sandra later had an overseas telephone conversation with him at which time he counseled her on additional training prior to opening our Inn. Overall, he was a fine gentleman and highly professional in his training and advice.

Sandra was also able to continue her training during her first year by herself in Vermont. Since I was gone so much of the time, she set up a temporary program of study at the Culinary Institute in Montpelier, Vermont. They offered a program where Vermont residents could participate in a series of one day demonstrations and lectures. The Institute was about one-and-one-half-hour drive north of us so Sandra would arise very early to make the trips to add to her knowledge base.

Following the completion of my Paris assignment and our move back to the U.S., I was on a cycle of frequent business trips to Paris over a five year period. On many of these trips, I would make a shopping visit at a favorite Paris cooking ware store. I would buy as much as I could reasonably carry of the copper pots and pans, recognized as some of the finest in the world. I would make my way through the airport duty-free lines with these purchases, and Sandra would use these for home entertaining, as she frequently prepared dinners for my business colleagues. This collection of fine cookware would go on to be used for her country inn kitchen.

Her single largest culinary educational experience came as we interrupted our efforts of renovating the Inn. You will read about this more completely in the next Chapter, but I am referring to this now, as it played a key role in Sandra's culinary development.

In the middle of our renovation experience, I was offered an IBM business assignment in London. This assignment allowed us two years in London immediately prior to my corporate retirement. While there, Sandra took the opportunity of attending a three-month program with a professional cooking school. IBM provided a very attractive retirement benefit program oriented to future retirees. They offered payment to employees and their spouses for courses aiding them in education toward retirement.

Sandra investigated different school possibilities and selected a program named La Petite Cuisine which had received high recommendations. The program featuring French cooking was intensive. It was three months in length, five days per week and required her catching a 7:00 a.m. train and returning home by 7:30 p.m. Armed with all her cooking instructions and a full book of recipes she was ready to go when we returned to Vermont.

After she finished her formal education program, she took on another individual training experience. Her friend and chef mentor,

John Desmond, had earlier suggested to her another possibility. That is, to work in a French Restaurant at no pay; the French term for that is "*stage*". That is what he, John, had done earlier in his life, and personally found it most productive for his training. He suggested a French friend of his that had a restaurant in London, and that Sandra should visit his restaurant and convince him she could be helpful in his restaurant.

Sandra was enthusiastic about this possibility, went to the restaurant, and began her request in French. The Chef switched to English, and was apparently impressed enough to agree for her to begin working in his kitchen for noon meals as a *Stage.* This was a three-month experience that ended because my assignment came to an end, and my retirement was about to begin. The final experience was a special dinner the Chef prepared exclusively in honor of Sandra, luckily to include me, for the time she had spent with him. Over the next several years, Sandra exchanged Christmas cards with the Chef and his wife.

The training experiences that Sandra had accumulated, developed into a highlight of the stay for our guests. She was responsible for the reputation that led to our Inn being named as a *Gourmet Getaway* in a special New England Guide to Country Inns. You will see a selection of her menus included in the chapter about the Opening of the Inn, as well as the recipes for the dishes she prepared for our Opening Dinner in the chapter, Inn Recipes.

A Major Change

A major change was about to take place.

Our Inn renovation work was proceeding at a good pace. The new heating system had been installed. But, while we had been making good headway on the renovations involving, carpentry, electrical and plumbing, we were finding we had far exceeded our original cost estimates, and were running low on money. On the IBM work front, my work and travel schedule was becoming far heavier which made the commuting more difficult for both Sandra and I. It was now almost one and one-half years since we had moved into our new life of me commuting and Sandra living in Vermont.

Over the past eight years including the time lived in France my job responsibilities had concentrated solely on Europe. I now found it necessary to further increase my business travel to Europe. My travel now began and ended in Vermont, which certainly lengthened the trips. Additionally, I had liaison and project management with a company in California recently added to my management responsibility. This now meant travel between our Vermont home, Europe and California with stops in our White Plains offices.

This increasing business responsibility combining IBM and the California company, caused a major organizational change for me that allowed Sandra and I to have the best of both worlds. IBM determined they should establish an independent business unit for Europe that would be headquartered in England. This would allow them to maintain a close relationship with the countries that were instrumental in their European marketplace, and to set up a telecommunications manufacturing facility in England. They would produce the new products from the development engineering that would be done by the company in California.

This change made it possible for me to accept a three-year business assignment based in London, England. The additional overseas assignment income would improve our personal funds for the renovation, and would allow the two of us to be together for more time again.

This experience of moving off to England was being made, oh so much easier, by the fact that our daughter, Laurie, had made the move back from Seattle. She had initiated and made the personal move, and had adjusted very well, so we were comfortable with leaving her by herself in this large unsettled house. She knew the projects that were being constructed and could handle any complexities, and if any difficulties, Sandra and I would be as close to Laurie as the telephone. We had seen how effective telephone communications could be to discuss and manage any open questions, so we were all happy. Ed would be checking in on a regular basis to see if Laurie needed anything, so our departure for London moved smoothly.

* * *

Life on a corporate assignment was not new, so we were able to make our plans with a minimum of fuss. We were not planning to move any furniture and would be renting a furnished apartment. We searched for a place to live and finally found an apartment (in British terms,"flat"). Elevators ("lifts") are not very common, so we decided a fourth floor walk-up would be good exercise. The flat was in Wimbledon, which is SW London and was an excellent location, convenient to the commuter train system, and all the conveniences we would need. In fact, we managed good seats for the Wimbledon Tennis Women's Singles Finals one year.

England was a superb assignment location for antique hunting in the many Antique Shops that are all over the Country. The Pubs are also a wonderful attraction and are even easier to locate than the Antique Shops. There are several individual published guide books, with good descriptions, for both antiques and pubs.. We would make a practice of making good use of these Guides. We would tour for antiques, and then would stop in one of the many pubs where we would have a classic pub lunch with a pint. This was an idyllic life, and we were able, over two years, to select antiques that we stored for shipment back at the end of our assignment. We also made some good acquaintances and located a master craftsman to fabricate some furniture for us.

We had been having difficulty finding a suitably large antique dining room table and chairs at a reasonable price. We were then lucky to find a shop right in Wimbledon near our flat that gave us a lead on a craftsman that would turn out to be a high point of our life in England. After a telephone call, we set up an appointment and made a driving trip to Northern Wales. Prior to our trip to Wales, Sandra and I had been on a recent overnight trip to Paris, and had spied a beautiful antique table in an up-scale Parisian Antique Shop. This was in the evening after dinner and the shop was closed, but the Shop was well lighted. I stood outside drawing a sketch which we then took with us on our driving trip to Wales.

Wales was nearly a full-day driving trip and we stayed overnight. The next day we visited Chris and his wife living in their stone cottage, dating from the Fourteenth Century, high on a rock covered hill (I think much of that part of Wales is rock covered). He was exceptionally accommodating and showed us examples of the contract pieces he had built. After viewing the sketch I had made of the table, he suggested he would draw some detailed plans and mail them to me in Wimbledon. If I liked them, he would begin work and I could send him a deposit. I had told him we were looking for a piece of furniture that appeared old, and we would prefer it to have a distressed appearance. He said he had just the wood for it. There had been a church over 200 years-old that had been razed some time back, and the 14 by 14 inch English Oak beams had been resting in water for years. They had enough length for the nine foot table we wanted.

Within a week, the drawings arrived and they were just what we wanted, so I mailed off the deposit amount. I had asked him to let me know before he was fully finished, so I could travel to see his work before possibly asking him for other pieces. He called me and suggested he was at a stage I should see before he finished. I made the drive and was completely impressed. He had not fully finished, in that it had just one coat of stain and was lacking any patina. But I wanted him to go ahead with the finishing touches and I was so impressed that I asked for some drawings for more pieces. My request was for Welsh Ladder Back Chairs with rush caned seats, and a seven foot long version of a Welsh Sideboard with Drawers and Doors, all to match with the table.

When he finished the table he arranged shipment by truck to Wimbledon. When the table arrived, we were, in today's vernacular, blown away. The patina was absolutely gorgeous and he included a can of the antique paste wax we would use to maintain the appearance. Over the years we continued to order the same antique wax made by an English company. His drawings for the chairs and sideboard arrived by mail, and again we were totally taken by his work, so I asked him to proceed. In time, these too arrived and they were equally gorgeous. They were from the same oak and also had some degree of distress, but to a lesser amount than the table.

We weren't finished yet. We were going to have a second dining room, the one that had been the original kitchen, but the room wasn't large enough for a similar sized table. We had decided we should have three separate pub-type tables, and they should be the same design as the large dining table but reduced in length and width. Additionally, for our last two pieces from Chris, we wanted a table for a TV Set to go into our library, so I designed a table that appeared as a shoe cobbler's work bench with cut-down short legs. This was also done with the very distressed wood from the beams. The last piece was entirely different and was a queen–sized headboard with spindles. Chris was excited as he said he loved to work with his lathe, and had a special supply of English Yew that finishes with a baby-smooth surface.

That was our last experience with Chris, and it was a totally outstanding relationship throughout. It marked the first, and possibly, last time that I completely trusted a business relationship, with so little direct contact. I recently tried to contact him by telephone from the United States. but, unfortunately, was unable to do so.

Then, we had a major stroke of good luck! I received word that IBM was considering the preparation of a large scale early retirement program as a way of cutting down the size of the work force. As with many rumors, there was no assurance this would happen, and the dates were unknown at that time. That would have fit in perfectly with my desire for early retirement, but you can't operate with rumors. I did find though that they would consider a special arrangement with some of the older management employees in the international operation I was with.

I pursued this, and as an older management executive, I found they were willing to negotiate individually with me. To shorten a story: my age made me eligible to meet the corporate policy for early retirement. I found they were agreeable to essentially buy me out with an offer that was just short of two years' salary, which would, happily, meet the amount we needed to pay for the finishing of the renovation effort. We shipped everything we had bought from Chris, as well as the antique accessory pieces from all the antique shops we had visited, back to Vermont in a container. Over the years since, we have sold or donated some of our antique pieces except for the work done by Chris. These are still with us, except for the few that are now with members of our family.

I would be less than honest if I said my job was the most important thought in my mind while we were living in England. The job did continue to keep me extremely busy, but fortunately I had been blessed by having a very good boss, Alan Willsher, and in selecting a very good international staff. When the opportunity was presented for me to leave at two years, it was an easy decision. Sandra and I toured Scotland with our son Jon, while everything was being packed into the container. We said goodbye to England and hello to retirement, and boarded our plane to return to the United States.

This was truly a major date for us. It was now one year beyond the target date we had set when we made the monumental decision to do the Country Inn. It was rather amazing that we were able to pull that off. It was also twenty-five years of being with IBM; years that I could look back with fondness and personal respect for having been a part of IBM's tremendous Corporate achievements. And the last milestone was a total of thirty-two working years when I added the seven plus years with AT&T prior to joining IBM.

As a self-congratulation: not bad for a guy, originally from Pocahontas, Iowa, born just at the start of the great depression. And, now this would be a start to an entirely different life with Sandra, who had lived with and supported me during our married years. We both had similar young lives that I believe equipped us for taking on this life style changing endeavor. Neither of us had any background in this type of life, but we had both always worked at part time jobs during high school and college life. Both of us had been in college fraternities which helped build the social skills so important to dealing with guests. Sandra is three years younger, so after I graduated college and served in the Marines, she finished her B.B.A. degree, magna cum laude, in three and one-half years. That was quickly followed by our wedding the day after she graduated, and we began the thirty two years leading up to this retirement day.

Finish Renovation

Laurie met us with the promise of an update on the most recent work that had been finished in time for our arrival. We were thrilled to see what had been accomplished, and realized that here we were in June with the outlook of finishing in time to open for our target date of Fall Foliage. Also, she happily showed us the wedding ring she had recently added to her left hand. She had married Darren, the young man we had met before we left for England, and told us they were going to be living just down the road in the Village. Laurie had just arranged a job with a nearby bank, and Darren would begin working for us, which was going to be a major help.

As Laurie proudly toured us through the projects she had been able to supervise with her crew of Amon, Bill and Gene we saw that the kitchen was ready for the chef's equipment to be ordered and installed. The dining rooms were ready for painting and for the new tables and chairs to be placed. This room with its large corner fire place, with the custom built table, chairs, and side board we were bringing back from England, would create a fine dining experience.

The second dining room had a new wood burning stove installed that was a pretty sight with its cherry-red enameled surface. The floor with its old bird's eye maple flooring had been refinished and clearly showed its antique character. The pub tables were going to fit perfectly with seating on antique chairs we were bringing back from England.

The kitchen construction had been finished so we could begin ordering the professional kitchen equipment. We installed a six burner gas stove with two ovens and a special construction exhaust system. She had two professional refrigerators. The dishwasher was state of the art and would wash a load in two-and-one-half minutes. There were more than adequate counters and a large center preparation space. The health inspector had required three sinks; one for pots and pans, one for vegetable prep and a separate wash-up sink. So we were ready to go.

Laurie then presented her Mom with a welcome back cookbook that became one of the favorites used over the years … and it still is. This treasured book, *The Victory Garden Cookbook by Marian Marsh* has contributed many excellent vegetable dishes to Sandra's menu selections.

As we finished our tour with Laurie, Sandra and I were able to see how close we were to finishing this total project. We jointly came to the conclusion that we could, with significant effort, meet our opening date of Fall Foliage. This gave us four months to go, and a new sense of enthusiasm.

This enthusiasm carried over, and into a quick start to find an Inn Dog. We had been thinking for some time, starting back in England, about getting a dog. We knew we wanted a puppy that would be grown by the time we opened for business. And, we wanted a large dog that both we and our Inn guests would love and remember. We hadn't yet settled on the breed we would have. We hadn't personally known Newfoundlands, or Newfies as they were known, but they had been highly recommended. We heard of one that was a champion and its owners were considering placing him with new owners, so we went to visit. We liked him, but the owners were having second thoughts, and they wanted to use him for breeding so he was not available at that time.

In retrospect, that was good for us. We found what we felt was the best dog in the world. Even today, while writing this memoir, I think about him and feel emotions for him. This lovely animal was a Bernese Mountain Dog breed, known by many as a Birner. He was a puppy, eight weeks old, one of two in his litter, and we fell in love with him. Fortunately, his owner recognized us as acceptable for him to live with. We named him Wimbledon, shortened to Wimble. Wimble grew into a beautiful, large dog, standing nearly twenty-nine inches and reaching a top weight of 145 pounds. The vet did then control us, and we kept his weight at 120. Wimble lived for nine and one-half years before passing away; unfortunately, many large dogs have shorter lives.

As an Inn Dog, Wimble was perfect. He had a coat that didn't shed. He was a dry-mouth dog in that he didn't slobber, and he didn't bark. He was respectful of people and was friendly without being energetic. A large dog of that weight could have been difficult if he jumped on people. The Bernese Mountain Dog breed originated in the mountains of Switzerland and was comfortable in the cold winters of Vermont. He was introduced to our home while all the building was continuing, so he grew up knowing heavy activity around him and was always relaxed.

The downstairs area had been the principal focus in our absence, so the upstairs renovation work still required quite a bit of work. Two of the bedrooms needed only cosmetic work so they were easy, and their bathrooms were also in good shape other than cosmetic. We now had to create additional bathrooms. Two of the bedrooms had closets that we could convert into small hallways. These opened into another former bedroom that with a new wall became the space for two bathrooms. Amon, our plumber, then applied his magic and developed two complete bathrooms. So far, that was four down, two to go.

Also upstairs, but in the other section of the house, we already had a bedroom with its own bathroom that needed modernizing, which was easy. The last one required some more imagination. This is the section that had the four dormitory style bunk bedrooms. We took those four individual rooms out and created a large bedroom with an elegant bath. The remaining space in that wing allowed us to build a bathroom for our owner's suite.

The front four guest bedrooms had the original staircase to and from the main living/dining area. This staircase was a match for the stairs in the court house in the Newfane, Vermont Town Square, and had an impressive appearance. The back two guest rooms had a staircase into the dining rooms. The owner's suite had its separate staircase to the office area off of the kitchen. All of the second floor rooms could access the external fire escape stairway.

While that construction work was being done, the painting and wall papering were also underway. We had the savvy help of our son, Jon, who had come up from New York to help us. Jon was an excellent painter artist with a fine sense of color and was especially helpful in advising us on painting and wallpaper. Additionally, he designed and painted a mural in an upstairs bedroom; this is the room that had a fireplace. The mural was a beautiful enhancement to this room with its corner window view across the pond, fields and distant, low, mountain range. As a final decorating touch, we used many of the fine paintings he had created to hang on our walls. The majority of them are still hanging on the walls of our current home.

Outdoors, we had also finished the parking area and walkways. Our original parking plan had been modified, but the walkway from the guest parking area would still have style in the way it was placed up to our guest entrance.

Opening

The first day of Fall Foliage dawned on us. We had been working at a high rate over the four months since we had returned from England and were at, probably, 98 percent complete. All of the features that would be critical to Guests comfort and expectations were complete. Sandra's menu was also complete and she was ready to perform.

Our work effort had been so all encompassing and focused on finishing construction that we hadn't attempted to do any marketing. One of the great advantages of aiming to open on the absolute peak visitor day of the year throughout the State is the overall abundance of visitors to the State. We were lucky because of two prime referral points that guided guests to our Inn. These were the local Chamber of Commerce, and another Inn that was most helpful.

Over the time we had been working on our property we had become personal friends with the owner of the top Inn in the area. With the outstanding reputation of his Four Columns Inn, Jacque Allembert had many more requests, plus drop-ins than he could handle, so he very nicely referred them on to us. We continued to be the beneficiary of his generosity over the next several months until we became popular enough on our own.

> ***Rule: Reach out to anyone who can possibly assist you in developing your market personality, and where possible to refer business to you. This does not necessarily require you to spend money on advertising, but it also does not mean you should not advertise. It means, develop your personality so that you benefit from personal referrals and word-of-mouth. If you have a Bed and Breakfast, be sure you are referring guests to restaurants, and that those restaurants know you are interested in them and will return the favor.***

Here we were: our opening day was very close to four years from the day we had made our offer to buy this wonderful property. As we showed the last of our guests to their room, Sandra and I breathed huge sighs of relief and told them dinner would be served at 7:30.

Dinner time at the Inn was normally at 7:30 p.m. with the fixed one time of serving, and the menu was always five-courses of a fixed menu. The menus would be varied from day to day and were chosen and prepared by Sandra. A selection of menus we used is shown later in this Chapter. Breakfasts were served between 7:00 a.m. and 9:00 a.m. and were also a fixed menu for the day. On this very special Opening Day, the Dinner Menu prepared by Sandra was:

Appetizer

Pochettes de Saumon au Fenouil

(Pockets (or Purses) of Salmon with Fennel)

Soup

Potage Cressionere
(Cream of Watercress Soup)

Entrée

Medaillons au Veau avec Sauce au Orange et Citron
(Filet of Veal with Sauce of Orange and Lemon)

Courgettes Farcie

(Zucchini Filled with Diced Onion,

Bacon, Tomato, Herbs and Seasonings)

Darioles de Betterave

(Small Moulds of Pureed, Creamed Beets)

<u>Salad</u>

(Fresh Market Greens)

<u>Dessert</u>

Poires au Vin Rouge

(Pears Poached in Red Wine)

Coffee or Tea

A Carafe of Wine with Compliments of the Inn

While the carafe of wine was complimentary, a wine list was available with a selection of Champagnes, White and Red Wines. Over time we found our house wines of either white or red were quite good, and popular, so not too many guests chose from the full List.

> **The decision to offer complimentary wine is one to consider carefully. As I have written, that offering is what we did, but there is no question in my mind that it definitely caused us to sell less wine from the list. It is natural that any free wine will encourage guests to accept the offering, and not go on to view other wines that were available and affordable. A suggestion is to offer a complimentary glass of wine before dinner, and have all dinner wines priced on the List. If you are offering a Wine List with priced wines, please**

investigate your local regulations regarding the need for a license to serve with your meals.

As a beneficiary of our extensive water development covered in an earlier chapter; we also found that our water was pure and fresh and made exceptionally good coffee and tea.

Sandra, of course, managed all the kitchen efforts with the support of a local woman who assisted beforehand in food preparation and kitchen clean-up following dinner. Bill served as a combination of Maitre'D, Sommeliere, and Garcon.

Our guests were made aware of the significance of this first dinner and were in full vocal accord with their appreciation of the occasion. They called Sandra in after dinner and offered their thanks with a hearty toast. It should be pointed out that our large table with guests clustered around gave a festive air, and the conversation among guests who had not known each other flowed openly. With the full house, the table was filled so the over flow as well as those guests who had the desire to dine by themselves were seated in the second dining room at the smaller tables.

The next morning Breakfast included:

Orange Juice

Milk

Coffee or Tea

Homemade Granola

Belgian Waffles with Pecans

Vermont Maple Syrup from Local Maple Trees

A Selection of Fruits

While we did find the variable breakfast time between 7:00 and 9:00 a.m. was good for some guests, we also saw there was interest in guests gathering at the same time around the large table to continue conversations. Throughout our time in business, the larger table groupings were highly positive. There were also some guests who did not care to join in group tables, so having the small tables with the intimacy they offered was a perfect solution. Our decision to have these tables made was certainly a good one. Interestingly, Sandra and I, just within this past year, traveled and stayed in a Bed and Breakfast that had the same type of table arrangements. The majority of the guests gathered at the group table, and the conversations were equally good to what we had always observed.

We congratulated ourselves for what turned out to be a successful opening for a Foliage season that lasted two weeks before tapering off, just as the foliage lost the brilliance of its colors.

Our Inn policy was two meals a day: Dinner and Breakfast. Sandra had found that all her training was paying off. Her exposure to the very many kitchen techniques and practices were invaluable in the original setting up of her kitchen. The actual selection of menus and cooking preparation became natural as she went about her daily tasks.

She had learned many new and creative approaches, and started putting them to work on a daily basis. The first order of business was to establish a series of dinner dishes that individually would be delicious to our guests. These would be *Appetizers, Soups, Entrees, Vegetables, and Desserts. Each dinner would also include a Salad making our total of Five Courses. The salad was typically of fresh greens and would be served between the Entrée and Dessert in the style we had become accustomed to while living in France.*

She had a repertoire of dishes she would use to select these evening dinner menus. It would be too much for this book to list all the individual recipes so I shall include a selection of menus for Dinners she has made. These are being listed by categories in the way she could combine them in different menus. These dishes have been selected from the different Cook Book sources she used; including *Ma Cuisine, John Desmond; La Petitite Cuisine School of Cooking*; *From Julia Child's Kitchen, Julia Child; The New York Times Cook, Edited by Craig Claiborne* and occasional personal sources.

Here are the Menu names for a selection of the wonderful dishes that emerged from Sandra's Country Inn kitchen. These are being shown in the major categories of: Appetizers, Soups, Entrees, Vegetables, and Desserts.

Appetizers

Vol au Vents aux Cailles

(Puff Pastry Basket with Filling of Quail, Shallot and Seasonings)

Quiche aux Champignons

(Flan with Bechamel Sauce and Mushroom)

Coueurs d'artichaut aux Oeufs et Sauce Beurnaise

(Artichoke with Poached Egg, Duxelles and Bearnaise Sauce)

Ouefs Poches aux Champignons

(Poached Eggs with Mushrooms)

Tarte a l'oignon Alsacienne

(Cream and Onion Tartelette)

Soups

Bisque Verte de Crabe and Avocat

(Bisque Of Crab and Avacado)

Crème de Champignons

(Cream of Mushroom Soup)

Potage de Poireaux

(Leek Soup)

Bisque de Crevettes

(Shrimp Bisque)

Entrées

Mignons de Filet de Boeuf avec Sauce Crème a la Moutarde

(Filet Mignon with Sauce of Dijon Mustard)

Sole Bonne Femme

(Sole With Shallots And Mushrooms)

Pochettes de saumon au fenouil

(Pockets of Pasta Sealed with Filling of Salmon,

Fennel, Onions and White Wine Sauce)

Tournedos Sauce Poivre Vert

(Filets with Green Peppercorn Sauce)

Paupiettes de Veau au Citron, Julienne de Carottes

(Veal Rolls with Lemon Stuffing and Carrot Julienne)

Poulet Poche, Sauce Estragon a la Julienne de Courgettes

(Poached Chicken with Tarragon Sauce and Zucchini Julienne)

Desserts

Poire Poche en Vin Rouge

(Pears Poached in red wine sauce)

Tarte Tatin

(Up-Side-Down Carmelized Apple Pie)

Crepes Roxelane

(Crepe with Sauce of Raspberry with Kirsch)

Souffle Froid au Citron

(Cold Lemon Souffle)

Souffle au Grande Marnier

(Grand Marnier Souffle)

Vegetables

Courgettes Farcies d'une puree de panais

(Zucchini Filled with Puree of Parsnip)

Gratin de Feuilles d' epinards

(Spinach With Mushrooms, Bacon And Shallots)

Gateau Moelleux de broccoli avec hollandaise

(Puree Of Broccoli In Dariole Mould With Hollandaise Sauce)

Asperges etuvees a la crème

(Asparagus Spears Simmered In Cream)

Aubergines Au Four, A La Provencale

(Eggplant Garnished With Fresh Tomatoes And Herbs)

Haricots verts a l'ail

(Green Beans Sauteed With Oil, Garlic, And Fresh Bread Crumbs)

Haricots verts a la provencale

(Green Beans With Tomatoes And Herbs)

Petits oignons a la grecque

(Little White Onions)

Celeri en branches a la grecque

(Celery Hearts Simmered With Oil, Lemon, And Herbs)

Tomates farcies a la provencale

(Tomatoes Baked With A Topping Of Herbal Crumbs)

Breakfast menus were not nearly as extensive, but the variety continued to be popular. There were basically three menus that were rotated including the Belgian Waffles already described. The Breakfast Entrees for each of the other days were Blueberry Pancakes and French Toast (or Pain Perdue). The accompaniments were the same as the other days.

For this memoir, and for those readers who like to see specific recipes, I am including the recipes Sandra used for the dinner dishes on our Opening Day. You will find them in the next chapter, Inn Recipes.

The practice we used in taking reservations was very helpful, in actual practice for some guests, and in relations with all guests. When we received telephone calls and gathered the specific guest information, we would always ask if any of the guests had any specific dietary considerations. On the occasional times, there was something to be avoided, we were able to vary the menu either for individual, or we could consider changing the menu dish for everyone to something else that was also delicious. This qualifies as a **Rule:**

> **Establish a policy that is always invoked at time of accepting reservations. Ask if any of the Guests have any dietary considerations the Inn should be aware of for any meals or snacks. Be as specific as possible. It can become very embarrassing if this is not determined until after food is placed on the table.**

This is a good time to offer some general observations we made on our guests. First, for the period covering our full time in business; our guests were, universally, great, and easy to get along with. Another observation is the make-up; i.e., personal profile of the guests. When I was doing my original "deep thinking" masquerading as market analysis, I thought more about the desires and habits of myself and my wife. I had been a large corporate type who had traveled a great deal, and we still enjoyed going off to stay in smaller Inns or B&Bs so I assumed this would be a market for our Inn.

Over time, I realized we were not drawing much from the business types I thought I knew so well. Our larger guest draw was from various types of professionals, both male and female. These included Medical Doctors from different disciplines ranging from general practice, to specialties and surgeons; academics from Elementary to University both teaching and administrative, Attorneys, Financial, Authors, and Technical. We would see those who were celebrating special occasions or who just wanted to get away from their normal life. In the winter we would see those that wanted to ski, but didn't want the busy life of a large ski resort. Summer was a popular time for guests who wanted to attend one of the musical programs that were available at concert venues.

Our greatest attraction for new guests was word-of-mouth advertising and repeat visits. Guests would pass on the news about our Inn to their friends who would be lead to call for reservations. They in turn would pass it on. Nearly equal in attraction were Guide Books; good articles in these books brought in new guests and then the word-of-mouth began to work. I prepared our country inn letterhead and brochure and used direct mail when I could find suitable groups, but I didn't find that was particularly successful.

The vicissitudes of the overall business environment had a significant effect on business. We found that the stock market crash of the Friday in October, 1987 had a major impact on our business. This was our second season and we were looking forward to building on the success of our beginning season. Fortunately, we had a good Fall Foliage season, but then after the stock market fall off we began to see reservations drop off. I don't believe there is much that Inns can do to offset this type of business hit, but be aware of the effect of circumstances that are beyond control.

At the time we were beginning, we had to be aware of AIDS. The subject of AIDS was becoming a national factor. Not too much was really known at the time, other than it was becoming a national health concern. We didn't know if we should take any special steps, and if so, what would they be? Basically, our approach was to be sure our private baths, cleaning, and laundry practices were as sanitary as possible. In retrospect, the national press provided helpful information, and we never felt concern from our guests. I believe, as a general rule, the guests that use Inns and/or B&B's are the types any of us would be pleased to have in our personal homes.

The matter of gays was also a factor in our thinking, albeit a minor one. The current national LGBT attention was not a factor at the time. We would occasionally have a gay or lesbian couple, but in our eyes as Inn Keepers there was never anything that reflected negatively. Again, as a general rule, the beauty of our Inn was the camaraderie of the guest's. The experiences with guests were nearly always the same as if we had invited friends who didn't yet know each other into our home for an overnight or weekend visit. They would socialize and when they wanted to, they would go out to pursue their own interests.

Our basic guest philosophy was to make our Inn as comfortable as possible for adults. Our policy was no children under age twelve, and at the time of making the reservations, parents would accept that without a fuss. We wanted our guests to look forward to the opportunity of being away from their home environment, to be able to fully relax, enjoy fine meals, enjoy being around other adults, and be sorry about having to leave at the end of their stay.

During our time, the internet had not yet been started. In today's hospitality industry, the internet is extremely powerful and useful. Websites have made such a strong mark on all businesses, but I believe the effect on Country Inns and B&B's is particularly strong. Tied together with digital photography, the website can exhibit the Inns to users in ways that could not be considered prior to the emergence of this phenomenon. Within this past year, Sandra and I used the internet to search for B&B's and selected our destination. We wished we had had this technological breakthrough during the days of our Inn. Adding the power of social media, there has indeed been a change for the better in this business.

Each Christmas, we would send out special cards to all our former guests. Our son, Jon, would prepare and draw a new design each year featuring some aspect of our Inn. These ranged from scenes of cross-country skiers, to scenes of the barn, to a decorated tree in front of the Inn with a warm message from Bill and Sandra. We always felt good about the personal message from the Inn. I should point out the value of return guests, and I believe cards such as these have a helpful hand.

While this following point may not meet the full category of a Rule: It is something that I believe should guide any that are thinking about this business.

> **Start making reservations to visit and stay at Inns or B&Bs, and make a practice of meeting as many of the guests as possible. Have conversations and learn about them and how they selected the B&B you are in. What are their plans while they are there? Learn as much as you can from your Hosts. Obviously, you do not want to become a nuisance, but you can be subtle; and you will benefit greatly.**

There will be times when family members and/or close friends have come to visit you at your Inn. This may be likely for important holidays or family occasions, and these guests will probably have expectations that might wish for more of your personal time or attention. Or it may be that you as Inn Keepers may wish closer connections with these guests. At times like these, you may also be having guests that have no close connection to you as Inn Keepers, and they will be expecting your normal friendly service.

The following **Rule** is included to cover that point:

Be aware that there may be times when you have your family members and/or good friends as guests at the same time you have other guests. It will be natural to have the situation when you as inn keepers may not be able to be with your close family/friends as you will be performing your role as host to paying guests. It can be a sensitive time regarding familial relationships.

Inn Recipes

As promised earlier, the recipes for the courses Sandra prepared for our ***Opening Dinner*** are presented here in detail, in the order in which they were served.

The ***Appetizer*** is a special concoction of Pasta and Salmon with Fennel topped with a sauce based on white wine and a fish stock. The pasta is prepared in the form of pockets, or some will call them purses. The salmon with a stuffing of Fennel, Onions and Cream is placed in the pockets, and topped with the sauce with a garnish of Dill. The name of this delightful dish is ***Pochetts de Saumon au Fenouil.***

The ***Soup*** is a classic and delicate with a subtle flavor based on Watercress. The name given to this soup was ***Potage Cressionere***.

The ***Entrée*** was a preparation of Filets of Veal cooked to perfection with a special sauce. The sauce is prepared with White Wine, Brown Veal Stock, Orange and Lemon Juices and Cream. The Garnish is segments of Lemon and Orange with a touch of Lemon Zest. The name of this dish is ***Medaillons au Veau avec Sauce au Orange et Citron.***

The ***Accompaniments*** are two ***Vegetables:***

The ***Zucchini*** is prepared and stuffed with a mixture of Diced Onion, Bacon, Tomato, Herbs, and Seasonings. The name of this dish is ***Courgettes Farcies.***

The ***Beets*** are served in the form of a Dariole Mould after being prepared with Cream, Orange Juice and Eggs, pureed and baked in the moulds. The classic deep red color of the beets presents a harmony of color for the entire meal. The name of this dish is ***Darioles de Betterave.***

The ***Salad*** is a mix of fresh green lettuces with an Inn dressing of Balsamic Vinegar and Virgin Olive Oil with seasonings. The salad is served in this order as it is believed that salads, following the main meal, help to ease the stomach.

Finally, the ***Dessert*** is one of our favorites. A Pear is peeled and cored, but leaves the stem. The pears are cooked in Red Wine with some Sugar, Cinnamon, Lemon Rind and Whole Black Peppercorns. The wine is reduced to a syrup and served with the Pear. You may wish to have it served with Brandy Flavored Whipped Cream or a scoop of Ricotta Cheese.

Potage Cressoniere

(Watercress Soup)

Ingredients

1/4	**C**	**Butter**
1		**Clove Garlic, Minced**
2	**C**	**Onions, chopped**
1	**Qt**	**Potatoes, raw, thinly sliced**
1	**Tbsp**	**Salt**
1/4	**tsp**	**Black pepper, freshly ground**
3/4	**C**	**Water**
1		**Bunch Watercress**
1 1/2	**C**	**Milk**
1 1/2	**C**	**Water**
2		**Egg Yolks**
1 /2	**C**	**Light Cream**

Serves 6 to 8

Heat the butter in a large sauce pan. Add the garlic and onions and saute until tender, about five minutes.

Add the potatoes, seasonings and 3/4 cup water. Cover and bring to a boil. Reduce the heat and simmer fifteen minutes or until the potatoes are almost tender.

Cut the watercress stems into 0ne-eigth-inch lengths. Coarsely chop the leaves.

To the potato mixture, add all watercress stems, half the leaves, the milk and water. Cook fifteen minutes. Puree in blender. Return to the saucepan and reheat.

Blend together the egg yolks and cream. Gradually stir into the soup and cook, stirring constantly, until slightly thickened. Garnish with the remaining watercress leaves and serve immediately.

Pochettes de Saumon au Fenouil

(Pockets of Salmon with Fennel)

Ingredients

PASTA		
3		**Eggs , 2 eggs for their yolks plus 1 egg**
1/3	**oz**	**Salt**
7	**oz**	**Flour)**
		Warm water optional (useful if making the pasta by hand
STUFFING		
1/3	**oz**	**Butter**
2	**oz**	**Fennel bulb, finely chopped**
2	**oz**	**Onions, finely chopped**
1	**Tbsp**	**Double Cream**
+ 2	**Tsp**	
		Salt & Pepper
2	**Tbsp**	**Fennel Seeds, crushed & sleeved**
4 1/2	**oz**	**Fresh salmon**
1		**Egg Yolk for sealing the pockets**
SAUCE		
< 1/2	**C**	**White wine**
> 2/3	**C**	**concentrated fish bullion**
1/3	**C**	**butter, unsalted, soft, in pieces**
+ 1	**Tsp**	**Lemon juice**
		Chives, handfull, finely chopped
3 or 6		**Sprigs of Dill for garnish**

Note:It is best to use Clarified Butter in sauce and stuffing.

Serves 6

PASTA

> **Mix the eggs and salt together to dissolve the salt. Place the flour and egg mixture in a food processor, and process until the mixture is grainy. Take it from the bowl and squeeze the dough into balls. (If you do not have a food processor, add a little warm water to the mix and form into dough.
> Rest for one hour.**

Mix the eggs and salt together to dissolve the salt. Place the flour and egg mixture in a food processor, and process until the mixture is grainy. Take it from the bowl and squeeze the dough into balls. (If you do not have a food processor, add a little warm water to the mix and form into dough. Rest for one hour.

Mix the eggs and salt together to dissolve the salt. Place the flour and egg mixture in a food processor, and process until the mixture is grainy. Take it from the bowl and squeeze the dough into balls. (If you do not have a food processor, add a little warm water to the mix and form into dough. Rest for one hour.

If possible, use a hand-cranking pasta machine for the next stage. (If you do not have one, roll out the dough very thinly.)

Set the rollers of the machine at their widest setting; i.e., the rollers are furthest apart. Divide the dough into four pieces and flatten into a rough rectangle. Cover the remaining pieces with an inverted bowl. Dust the dough with flour, and feed it through rollers. Fold the dough in half and feed it through the rollers 8 or 9 times more, fold it in half each time. Repeat with the other pieces of dough.

Turn the dial to lowest notch. Feed the dough through the rollers without folding. Repeat with the remaining strips of pasta. The pasta should now be in long smooth strips. Place on trays lined with tea towels and cover with cling film. (If you have rolled the pasta by hand, cut it in half. Bear in mind that 6 pockets (purses) must be obtained). The pasta may be left at this stage.

STUFFING

Place the butter in a small frying pan with the fennel and onions. Fry gently, add the cream. Reduce until a thick mixture is obtained. Season.

When the ingredients for the stuffing are ready, stamp out 12 ovals from the pasta using a fluted oval cutter 5 ½ inches (13.5 cm) long. Paint the ovals with egg yolk. Place two small teaspoons of fennel and onion mixture on six ovals, and cover with the slice (s) of salmon. Season. Add a pinch of the crushed fennel seeds.

Cover with the remaining 6 ovals and press to seal I/5 inch (1/2 cm) from the outer edge, using a smaller oval fluted cutter upside down 4 ½ inch (10.5 cm) in length. The little pockets (purses) can be kept in the refrigerator on a tea towel lined tray until required. They can be prepared well in advance. (If you do not have an oval cutter, round cookie cutters may be used with equal success.

SAUCE

Boil the white wine and fish stock in a pan (not aluminum) until reduced to 5 fluid ozes (150 ml). Then add the butter a piece at a time and whisk vigorously until smoosth. Season, and take off the heat. Add lemon juice to taste and add chives.

TO FINISH

Meanwhile bring a large stock pan of water to the boil, and add 2 1/2 Tbsp (50 ml) of salt. When water is at rolling boil, and you have just made the sauce and prepared the garnish, add the pockets (purses) to the water. Cook in boiling water for two minutes until pasta is soft and wrinkled. Lift out with sieve, drain well, place quickly on paper towel, then on individual plates. Pour sauce over pockets (purses). Garnish each plate with a sprig of dill.

Serve immediately.

Medaillons au Veau Avec Sauce au Orange et Citron

(Filets of Veal With Sauce of Orange and Lemon)

Ingredients

8		Trimmed Veal Filets - 2.75 oz
1.4	oz	Butter - Clarified
< 1/2	C	White Wine
> 3/4	C	Brown Veal Stock
<1 1/4	C	Double Cream
1		Lemon - segmented and juice
1		Orange - segmented and juice
		A little zest of lemon and orange
		Salt and freshly ground pepper

Serves: 4

Trim the filets to size, season and saute in a little buster until just cooked and golden brown. Remove from pan.

Add the white wine to the pan with the brown veal stock to deglaze the pan, add a little orange and lemon juice, and reduce quite slowly by approximately a half.

Add cream, reduce slowly to required consistency, check seasoning and adjust to taste with salts, pepper, lemon juice and orange juice.

Arrange the meat on serving dish, coat with the sauce and garnish with lemon and orange segments and a little zest.

Courgettes Farcies

(Zucchini Filled with Diced Onion, Bacon, Tomato, Herbs and Seasonings)

Ingredients

4		**Zucchini - Medium**
<1.75	**oz**	**Clarified Butter**
1		**Small Shallots - finely chopped**
3 1/2	**oz**	**Bacon - unsmoked, with most fat removed**
1		**Tomato - large, skins, seed, juice removed**
1	**tsp**	**Fresh Herbs, plus extra for garnishing**
		Salt and Pepper

Serves 4

Peel the Zucchini lengthwise in strips. Trim ends. Scoop a hollow trough lengthwise in each zucchini and check that the zucchini stands without rolling.

Blanch and refresh the zucchinis. Melt the butter and cook onion gently for 5 minutes. Finely chop (or mince) the bacon, add to pan and cook for further 10 minutes. Add tomatoes coarsely chopped, herbs and seasoning. (Careful with the salt) and pile into the zucchini.

Place into a buttered oven dish. Transfer to hot oven, 400° F, (200° C) for 5 to 10 minutes until hot and bubbling. Garnish with fresh herbs and serve.

Darioles de Betterave

(Small Moulds of Pureed, Creamed Beets)

Ingredients

7	**oz**	**Beets- Cooked, without greens**
1/3	**C**	**Single Cream**
1	**Tbsp**	**Orange Juice, Concentrated)**
plus 1	**Tsp**	**" "**
2		**Eggs**
		Soft butter for moulds
		Salt and White Pepper

Serves 4

Line a small roasting tray with a double sheet of greaseproof paper which has a cross cut through it. (This stops the dariole moulds floating.) Cut the beet into pieces and puree with cream and orange juice in a food processor until completely smooth. Add the eggs and process again. Season.

Pour the mixture into 4 buttered dariole moulds. The mixture should come halfway up in the moulds. Place in the roasting tray of boiling water and cook in a preheated oven of 350° F, (180°C).

Cook for 30 minutes, then rest in a warm place for 5 minutes before turning out onto plates.

Note:It is best to use Clarified Butter in sauce and stuffing.

Note: If cooked longer than 30 minutes, beets will turn russet in color. The acidity of the orange juice holds the red color. This is true for red vegetables.

Note: Dariole Moulds may not be a part of your kitchen. If you wish to buy them, you may try Amazon.com. Or you may serve to plate with serving spoon.

Note: The size of the dariole moulds in this receipe was 1/2 inch deep by 2 1/2 inches wide. Sandra used small ceramic egg cups to make hers. This dish was used as a garnish to give color.

Poires au Vin Rouge

Pears Poached in Red Wine)

Ingredients

1 1/2	L	Red Wine
1	C	Sugar
1		Cinamon Stick
1		Rind of Lemon
5		Whole Black Peppercorns
8		Pears

Serves 8

Put Red Wine into large saucepan with sugar, a cinnamon stick and the rind of 1 lemon. Bring to a boil.

Peel 8 pears, leaving the stem and removing the core Put the pears into the saucepan with the wine. The wine should cover all the pears; if not, add a little water. Cook gently. When a fork will pierce the pears without any resistance, take the saucepan off the heat and let it cool. Remove the pears and let cool. Reduce down the liquid over high heat until slightly syrupy.

Add whole black peppercorns and cook another 10 minutes. Let cool. To give extra flavor to the sauce, the lemon may be squeezed after zesting and the juice added to the wine liquid before serving.

To arrange the dish, put each pear in the middle of a plate with some sauce around it.

This dish may also be accompanied by brandy flavored whipped cream. Another delicious approach is to substitute the whipped cream with a scoop of Ricotta Cheese.

The Inside Story

Thus far, I have written about our efforts in the actual creating of the Inn, as well as some of our unusual experiences and outside activities. However, this description of our Inn would not be complete without knowledge of some of our operational experiences. I am going to write about these, though they are principally, my view of, Sandra's inside-the-Inn operational responsibilities. I have, of course, consulted with her in writing this.

Staffing became very important. Sandra worked it out, so that she would have part time help. Normally, there would be one person to help her in the dinner prep work, and then to help with clean-up after dinner. She would also have a part timer come in the mornings to help with the rooms and other household tasks. The locating and hiring of these helpers became a story.

This was late morning on a day shortly after we had our opening day, and just after guests had departed. Sandra had been thinking about the need to hire someone part time, and she was just walking into the main dining room. At that precise moment, an antique corner cabinet, housing an antique tea set began to slide down the wall. We had apparently done an inadequate job of mounting it during our furniture set up activity. Sandra, who had been carrying some dishes in one hand saw this, and was able to use her free hand to stop the sliding of the corner cabinet. Here she was, keeping the antiques from falling to the floor and breaking, stuck with being unable to move, and too far away to put the dishes she was holding on the dining table to save them.

At that moment, Molly walked in the door and came to her rescue. After the dishes were placed on the dining table, and Molly helped Sandra with the rescue of the antique cabinet, they both heaved a big sigh of relief. Sandra asked Molly why she was there, Molly replied "I'm looking for a job."

"You're hired," Sandra responded with a hug. They worked out the arrangement of part time, which was acceptable to Molly, and she began in the kitchen with Sandra the next day.

During our years of operating, Sandra had a total of four regular women alternately helping her with tasks I already mentioned: dinner prep, dinner clean-up, plus rooms and bathrooms, and general household tasks. If one of the regulars would be off for a period of time, Sandra would have a substitute fill in. The reputation of the Inn and particularly of Sandra made it rather easy to find substitutes. The tourism and hospitality industry in Vermont employ a large number of Vermonters so there were always trained people available from a general pool.

The two employees who were with us the longest time were Jane and Randi, who became good friends with Sandra, and looked to Sandra as rather like family. Randi became pregnant, and when time came she asked Sandra if she would drive her to the Hospital to be with her during birth. Sandra drove Randi and her teenage daughter to the hospital, and both were there to witness the birth of her new daughter. Jane was an even stronger family association as we socialized with her and her husband, Bob, on multiple occasions. We were later honored to be invited to their daughter's wedding. We recently heard that Jane had passed away and was followed by Bob, so we lost two friends over a short time.

Jessica, a high school student, always brought a youthful enthusiasm to the kitchen, and worked only in the afternoon after her classes. She was taking French and because of Sandra's experience of living in Paris, she was especially helpful to Jessica's high school study. During the time of working for Sandra, Jessica went with her class on a trip to Paris, and was so entranced with French that she eventually moved to France to live and teach English. Jessica had bought a special prom dress on her Paris trip, and on the night of her high school prom she brought her date to have a picture taken in front of our fireplace.

Our kitchen was well equipped and spacious so that the helper who was on duty had a separate prep room. This room provided work space outside the heat of the kitchen, and was just right for working with pastries. The previous owners had left a separate large piece of marble, a slab, on the counter top in this room that worked perfectly.

Sandra managed all the cooking and the women would give her help in preparing the attractive plates for each course for me to take into the tables for the guests.

As the guests finished their various courses, I would bring the dishes into the kitchen. The helper would clear them off and place them into the dishwasher. This was a heavy duty top-of-the-line commercial product, and could wash a load in two and one-half minutes. The water was highly heated and the steaming, hot dishes were taken out as soon as the load was complete. We had special trays that the clean dishes were then placed in and moved to a drying rack that held up to four of these trays. Because of the heat of the water, the dishes would dry very quickly.

At the conclusion of the evening, I would take the dishes out to the dining room and place them back in the sideboard we had brought from England. When we lived in England, we did more than search for antiques and furniture. Sandra and I had visited Poole Pottery where they produced all manner of tableware, and we bought two full twelve piece place and service settings.

We acquired our place settings of silverware from IBM. IBM had a policy of awarding employees, in appreciation of their reaching twenty-five years of service, with a selection of meaningful gifts. I coincidentally qualified with the length of service at retirement, and chose a full twelve piece place setting of silver. I also requested the opportunity of purchasing, at my expense, an additional similar set of silver. This was granted, so we now had the silver and dishes we would need for the Inn. The sideboard was a perfect fit in our dining room and all the dishes, silver, glassware, table place mats and napkins were also a perfect fit.

When we were in our final two months before opening, Sandra said we had to make arrangements for some sewing that she wasn't going to have time to do. She asked Dave, our realtor, if he had any ideas who could do some sewing for us locally. He immediately told her about a business down in our village; a couple who operated out of the barn behind their house and made down comforters and terry cloth bathrobes. Sandra went to see them and was pleasantly surprised to see the range of their products.

We had them make several different and very useful items for us: down comforters for each guest room bed, very comfortable terry cloth full bathrobes for cold weather use for all guests, place mats for the dining tables, and napkins. The robes were especially good, and we had them made in two colors. We had an attractive raspberry color for women and deep blue for men. In addition to the cold weather bathrobes, we also had light weight robes Sandra and I had brought back from Bali. We had vacationed in Bali several months earlier while still living in England and had looked ahead; these were not exactly Vermont style but very practical.

Either Jane or Randi, depending on schedule, came in to work normally just after breakfast as guests were checking out. They would help Sandra begin the room and bath cleaning. Clean bed linens and towels were stored in linen closets and easily accessible. The used linens and towels were taken down to the laundry and into the washing machine as soon as guests left. On the very busy holiday weeks, we found it was more practical to go into town and use a commercial laundromat. On these same weeks, there was a greater need for additional grocery shopping so Sandra would combine the two.

Sandra's helpers would also assist in the general household cleaning tasks of sweeping, dusting, straightening and any other miscellaneous needs. One task that always had a nice result and appearance was the buffing of the furniture pieces we had brought back from England. These pieces, particularly the nine foot long dining table and the sideboard, had a beautiful patina that we would refresh periodically through use of the antique furniture wax we brought back with us. These pieces were also frequently buffed which added to their mellow appearance.

Another daily requirement was to clean the ashes out of the fireplaces in the living room, dining room, library and the one guest room. The fire was laid in preparation for lighting later in the day when we had guests. We had screens for all fireplaces, so these had to be properly closed after each cleaning. In addition to these fireplaces, we had the attractive wood stove in the second dining room that also required cleaning and preparation for the next fire lighting.

Sandra managed her grocery shopping trips based on her needs as dictated by her menu planning. She would identify the products she would need, and where necessary, from experience, would call the stores and speak to the individual department managers to place her orders. This close communication became very helpful as she built up a close respect and relationship, and the managers became comfortable in offering suggestions on their products. The fish store, mentioned previously, and the meat department of the super market were very accommodating.

There were two weekly deliveries to the Inn that were very beneficial. Friday deliveries were convenient to meet the need of weekend dinners. The Green Grocer truck had outstanding vegetables and lettuces always superior to super markets. Another truck delivering commercial restaurant supplies was most welcome for large rolls of parchment paper, aluminum foil and plastic wrap. She still has some of those rolls in her cupboard today.

A last delivery that was important to our operation was that of Wine and Beer. We established a good relationship with a Vermont distributor of alcoholic beverages. With his professional expertise and recommendations we prepared a varied wine list with selections ranging from good to fine. I also followed his pricing recommendations. Deliveries were made once a month.

Special Weekends

Weddings were a special time for our Country Inn, but some words of caution may be worthwhile. First, a reason to encourage weddings is the business you will receive. Of course, there is also the sentiment and emotion from seeing the happiness of couples united in matrimony. I'll begin with the highlight of our Inn wedding experience.

The Country Inn was turned into a magical setting for a snow covered wedding over the long New Year's weekend, and the pond was featured as one of the highlights for the wedding party. Planning for this weekend started back in late summer when we received a telephone call from a young lady saying that she had grown up coming to parties given by the previous owners of the home that was now the Country Inn. She had such fond memories of the good times, with sledding in the snow that she wanted to recreate those times and be married at the Inn. Her Mother and Father would book all the rooms in the Inn for the three day New Year weekend. This would involve an outdoor play-in-the-snow afternoon, breakfasts and dinners, the wedding and reception for guests and additional friends.

We thought this could be a truly special wedding and enthusiastically agreed to be the hosts. Outdoor preparation around the pond would require extra special effort. When the bride-to-be was coming as a child, the level of sledding and play at that time was not going to be suitable for the today's adults at the wedding. Darren and I went to work and cleared off a hill that was steeper and longer next to the pond. We cut and split firewood for a large bon fire at the edge of the pond.

The parents and close relatives had come in early on the day before the wedding to enhance the special decorating Sandra had begun. Later in the day, the bride and groom to be and other close friends and relatives arrived for cocktails and then out for a family dinner. The next day as the family continued their preparations, Darren prepared the pond for skating later that day by clearing the ice. The wood pile was ready for the match to light the fire.

There is one particular scene that will dwell in our memories forever, and illustrates the scenic wonder of this Inn. Just as guests began to arrive in the late afternoon for the planned outside play activities, it began to snow with large, fluffy flakes. There was no wind so that it quickly added fresh, white depth to that already on the ground. From the windows of the Inn you would look down on what could be realistically described as another Currier and Ives scene.

The pond ice had been cleared of snow and was active with ice skaters twirling on the ice. Next to the pond was the large bon fire with wedding guests warming themselves. On the slope down from the country road there were guests sledding from the road past the pond into the flat field where they cruised to a stop. They would then climb back up the hill for another run. Beyond, there was a horse drawn wagon on skis loaded with guests circling the snow covered fields. This was a magical beginning for such a special weekend.

After the play period, and guests had retired to their rooms to prepare for the wedding, the entire wedding party assembled. The wedding ceremony was conducted in front of the living room fireplace with all the guests gathered around. Sandra had prepared a wonderful assortment of foods that were presented in the dining room, and guests settled in to the many sofas and chairs to eat and enjoy themselves. Champagne toasts followed and the reception party began with wine, champagne and dancing. Guests with rooms at the Inn danced until they retired to their rooms. The following morning after breakfast they bade their goodbyes and departed. It was so special for the Bride and Groom that they returned the following year to spend their first anniversary over the New Year with us. On occasions like this, we would add extra help; Laurie and a very good friend, Tony Brennan, volunteered.

This was a wedding that went by the book; it was happy, the Inn received full occupancy, the Wine List was fully utilized, and payment was in full.

Later in the summer we had another wedding with essentially the same format. We had the same committed arrangement of booking all rooms of the Inn for the wedding party and family, with all meals including the wedding dinner and wine and champagnes, but there was a major difference. The bride and groom skipped on us by paying with a fraudulent credit card. This is a critical **Rule:**

> **When committing yourself to a major production, be sure the method of payment is checked thoroughly. And investigate the parties in advance to determine their reliability. If you are tying up your Inn for a particular occasion, obtain references and secure a substantial deposit. In these days of scams, you cannot be too careful.**

To show the variety possible for special occasions, we had another wedding of a local couple we had befriended. They had what I will describe as a country wedding. Their guests were escorted to a location on the field where they waited for the bride and groom with their attendants to walk to a knoll for the ceremony. The knoll allowed a view across the fields and could be seen from the windows of the Inn. They had their individual ceremony, and then all moved back to the pond where a colorful large tent had been erected for the reception. As with other special weddings, the Inn had been reserved for the weekend for the families of the bride and groom.

The Decision

Six days a week, either Sandra or I would go down to the Post Office in the Village with Wimble on his leash, to check our box for mail. This was always a good occasion to see folks we would normally not see in the course of our Inn activities, pass a few pleasantries, and catch up on any local highlights.

After picking up the mail, we would stop at the village general store. We had a good friend who owned the store, and who always enjoyed seeing us. He and his wife had two young school age children, and we were always interested in hearing any news of them. He would always pass on any local gossip so we could be current about happenings in the village. After a few minutes of conversation, Sandra, who had the mail run that day, continued on home with Wimble.

Back at the Inn, I came in for lunch from my job of splitting wood in preparation for the coming winter. This was always an activity that took several days to lay in the winter supply. I would arrange for delivery of a load of logs to be dropped out behind the Inn where I would cut them to fireplace length with my chain saw. The next step would be to split them with my log splitter and stack them in neat rows four feet high by eight feet long in the covered racks attached to the back of the kitchen L. My goal was to produce four cords, and if I would need more later in the winter I could buy them already split from Brent.

Sandra handed me the mail before lunch saying, “There is a letter from the Internal Revenue Service that you should look at.”

“OH, I better sit down before I do that.” I sat down and opened the letter and started reading. “This says they want to see us. I am going to call Sheldon after lunch so he can advise us how to handle this.”

Sheldon, or Shel as he was known, was a long-time friend, CPA and tax advisor. He had been preparing our income tax returns for many years. After lunch, I called Shel, explained what we had received, and then after more discussion I faxed a copy of the IRS letter to him. We planned in our telephone conversation that we would talk again in two days.

Sandra and I then sat down to begin our discussion on how to best proceed. We did have guests expected to arrive later in the afternoon but we would have some time now.

"Sandra, this IRS letter is to be expected. Shel and I have talked about this before and knew we would be hearing at some time. We have had business, but not nearly enough income to offset our costs so far in our nearly three years of operation as an Inn. We haven't paid Federal taxes during that time, and we know the IRS expects us to make a profit.

"What can Shel do to help us?" Sandra asked.

"He is going to call back in two days," I responded. He will plan on coming up here after he sets a date with the IRS auditor. He will show the auditor, at that time, that we have done nothing illegal and can explain our business situation."

"But, won't we have to have a plan to show how we can move our business to a level where we have enough income to show a profit. And if that is possible why haven't we done it before?" asked Sandra.

"I know this is difficult! You and I have talked about this many times. We are just too small. We have found that with our limited number of six rooms, we don't have the capacity that would pull enough income even during our peak business times. Either we raise the attic roof and convert it to more rooms, and/or we expand the restaurant and open it to the public."

"Bill, you're right we have talked about this and we have always reached the same conclusion. That is something that is quite difficult, and is outside and above our initial desire for this business."

Sandra and I had discussed this as we were going through the details of our renovation planning soon after we had moved in. We had also had a conversation with a consultant who specialized in country inns and B&B's. The general consensus was that eight rooms would be optimum as a business for the two of us to operate. Ten or more rooms would be at the point where we would need to hire additional staff to operate.

While it may have been technically possible to expand and convert the attic into guest rooms and baths, the amount of money we ended up spending on the renovation had already put us in the hole. Spending even more money didn't seem to be a wise decision. The idea of expanding the kitchen and dining room had also been a part of our discussion, but the need for additional staffing would have taken this out of the scope of the family operation we were comfortable with.

"Let's give this some overnight time and more thought. It's nearly time for our guests to arrive."

After a leisurely breakfast the next morning, the guests took a walk down to the river. After that, they spent some time chatting with us before checking out of their room and leaving for their next Vermont destination.

We then sat down to continue our discussion of yesterday about how to proceed with our IRS situation. As so often can happen with two married people when they have a joint problem that is truly serious, we had both thought of a possible solution. We both believed we were living a good life, thoroughly loved the local environment and wanted to continue living there as long as practical.

The total land of 115 acres was far more than necessary for the Inn. Our thinking had progressed to the idea of building a house for ourselves on a portion of the land, and selling the Inn with the remaining property. If we did this, we were sure the sale of the Inn and land could bring enough profit that the IRS would receive a satisfactory tax return. We could easily subdivide a seventeen acre section that was naturally separated by the stream bed near the barn down to the river, and build a home for us.

We agreed this could be a wise decision, but before we would call Shel we would discuss this with a local realtor. I decided to consult a particular realtor because her firm was affiliated with Sotheby

International Realty. In addition to their famous auction house they had a network of brokerage agencies, international and domestic, who specialized in high market value properties. The improvements Sandra and I had made in the property now made it especially attractive on the high end of the Vermont real estate market.

I placed a telephone call to the realtor who was enthused at the prospect of handling the property, and promised to call Sotheby immediately to set up a visit. She called back within the hour to say she had arranged to have the vice president make a trip from New York, and they would come to the Inn to explain the marketing program they could put in place. A date was set up, and as I finished that call we felt a financial burden could have been lifted from our shoulders.

Our next call was to Shel who was equally pleased with the plan. It was agreed that he would set up a date to fly north to visit the local IRS office after the property had been officially listed, and the marketing program materials were available. His plan was to convince the IRS they should not pursue any action at that time as their prospects of a higher tax return were significantly greater with this marketing plan. He expressed confidence this would work.

Things now moved quickly. A listing contract, with its special marketing program and commission arrangements, was agreed upon. Arrangements were made for the Sotheby photographer to visit within a week. The resulting professional glossy brochure presented the outstanding Inn in the best light, and they began distributing the listing materials through their local, national, and international channels.

Shel handled the arrangements for an appointment with the local IRS office, and soon he arrived to spend two days with us. It was good to see our friend again, but the circumstances made us anxious. He calmed us down and assured us we had everything needed for the meeting with the Sotheby marketing materials we were using. Later, over a lunch prepared by Sandra, he told us the meeting had gone according to plan. The IRS had been satisfied with the information, the marketing program and the expectation of the sales price and potential tax revenue.

We remained open for business while the Inn was on the market. The task that most people have when selling a house is that of always keeping it neat and ready to be shown. In our case we would be neat at all times, as we would continue to have guests as normal. Most of the prospective buyers would be shown through by realtors, and they would primarily come during the day when our room guests were out touring. Thus we had very little concern about contact between prospects and guests, and didn't have to worry about impact on business.

We did have one significant visitor that came to see the Inn soon after we had listed it. We were most pleased to make the acquaintance of the great granddaughter of the gentleman who bought the house and property in 1945. Her great grandfather was the New York banker who, along with his sister, had modernized the house and brought it into the Twentieth Century. She inquired about the possibility of having a family reunion, date unknown at that time, but within this next year. After discussion, she understood that although we were enthusiastic about having her family reunion at the Inn, we could not guarantee being open on this unknown future date. Our primary motive was a sale, and she couldn't take the chance of the Inn selling and having to cancel her family's plans. We parted after a pleasurable visit and a tour through her old family home, and showing her all of the changes.

The reason this plan to sell came together as quickly as it did is that when we had made the original decision to buy this property, we had thought about back-up plans in case of financial need. We had realized that with the combination of its size and beauty, the property was valuable for its future potential of subdivision and development. We did not buy with the intent to subdivide, but were comfortable with the idea if it should become necessary.

After we had finally opened for business, I had begun thinking about the future of our land. I engaged a land surveyor and had him survey the total property with an eye toward understanding the future possibilities. The conventional wisdom on subdividing was to do so in ten acre lot sizes. As I looked at the professional survey results, and with my increased knowledge of the property topography, I felt ten acre lots wouldn't be the best use of the land. It appeared that with the layout of the land, a minimum of fifteen acres would probably be better. I didn't file the survey with the Town, but just kept it in my personal files.

At the time we were ready to place our Inn for sale, we also sold a fifteen acre piece of land that was nearly one-half-mile up the road and not at all visible from the Inn. A couple who were just retiring wanted to build a home, so we closed on that land transfer.

Sandra and I did not want to move away following sale of the Inn, so we followed through on our plan and, further subdivided land for our home across the road near the barn and the river. This was approximately a seventeen acre piece of land that was perfect for us. I would prepare any ACT 250 submissions that were necessary for any of this subdivision activity. That still left the Inn to be sold with eighty-three acres. Approximately forty-two of these acres were on the Inn side of the road across from the barn.

It had become very obvious to us, that the Country Inn property would most likely not sell as a commercial venture. The problem we had had was going to be true for whoever might buy it. The size of the Inn, namely six guest rooms, was not large enough to create the revenue flow necessary to support the loan most buyers would have to have.

We had felt that the best sales market would be individuals or families that had the discretionary capital to use this fine building and property as a home or leisure estate. We found there was good interest, and before long we had a cash offer, very close to our asking price, that we accepted. This was to be used by the buyer's family as a vacation home with their primary interest in proximity to the nearby ski areas. In addition to the real estate sale, we also negotiated with them for their cash purchase of most of the Inn furnishings, and felt we were on track for an early closing.

Unfortunately, the buyer's attorney recommended termination of the sales contract, because the Vermont Act 250 requirements would affect the buyer's future actions for further subdivision. This is not to say he wanted to subdivide, but the onerous ACT 250 process, considering the price he was paying for the property, was more than he wanted to take on. Consequently, he made a sales price counter-offer to me that was far lower than we would accept, so we parted company. This is another example of ACT 250 becoming a significant problem.

Another offer was received soon after this one that reinforced the value of the property as a personal residence. In this case, the potential buyer was Ron Howard, former movie youth actor, now a well-known Hollywood Director/Producer. He and his wife visited the property and were thrilled with it. The one concern they expressed was the proximity to the road. The vehicular traffic had never been a problem to us, but they were worried about the stream of people they knew would be coming to the door just to meet them or get autographs.

The next day, the buyer's real estate agent called for an appointment and stopped later that day. She explained how much her clients liked the house and wanted to make an offer, which she did. The amount was nearly acceptable, and with some negotiation could probably have been arranged. But, she said, the offer was dependent upon moving the house across the road to a lower field where it would not be so easily accessible to passersby. In answer to my question, she said, we as sellers would be responsible for paying the cost of the moving. She was told no, and we ended her visit.

You would have to understand the construction of the house and the difficult terrain over which it would be moved to understand the country expression: "*you can't get there from here.*" Perhaps in the mind of a famous Hollywood Director/Producer they can do anything. This couple eventually found another very nice property on a back road outside our village and bought it for a vacation retreat.

After that experience, we continued to have lookers, but they were mostly folks who wanted to have the dream of owning a Country Inn or Bed and Breakfast. The financial numbers would not work for those who got to the point of discussing bank loans.

While this was happening, we continued to operate the Inn with guests. After some months, a husband and wife couple were shown through the property by one of the brokers affiliated with the international agency we had selected a year earlier. The buyers were the right combination: a couple that wanted to locate in Vermont, live in a nice property and operate their business from their home.

The Sotheby broker, Ruth, rather amazingly, had been the Inn Keeper of an Inn near Killington, Vermont that Sandra and I had stayed at several times during our earlier skiing days. As a matter of fact, during the period when we had first looked at the property, we had hooked up with her over dinner to discuss Inn Keeping. She had since left her Inn for a career in real estate.

After a delay of a few weeks Ruth returned with the couple to look again, and shortly thereafter opened negotiations with an offer. The price we were asking was higher than they felt they wanted to manage, so we suggested we could accept a reduced price by detaching the acreage across the road from the sale. Further, they could retain right of first refusal on that acreage, should we decide to sell it at some time in the future. This was acceptable and was written into the contract, and the Inn was finally sold one year from the date we had originally placed it on the market.

The final sales price of the reduced acreage of the property was substantially higher than our purchase price of the original total property. The profit and resulting income tax payment was very healthy for the IRS, but perhaps not surprisingly, we never received a thank you note from the IRS.

The sale of the Inn was eight years from the time of our attendance at the Vermont Wedding, and the beginning of the marvelous adventure. In summary, though operating the Inn was not financially acceptable, from our viewpoint it was very stimulating, satisfying and personally rewarding. The delay in selling the Inn was longer than we expected, but the timing of the final sale resulted in our completion of the new house. We were able to move into the house the day before the closing on the Inn.

This was a great and celebratory time.

Our New House

This chapter on building our replacement house will have little connection to the story about creating our Country Inn, except that it will further demonstrate our love for this property.

Sandra and I continued to own all the land on the barn side of the road, including the seventeen acre parcel where our new house was under construction. As soon as we had listed the Inn, we began planning to build a house on this piece of land near the barn. We had no idea how long it might take to sell the Inn, but we did know we were ready to begin.

The new house location was about 500 feet away from the Inn on the other side of the road, just down from the barn in the direction of the village. As described earlier, when we had originally prepared the market listing for the Inn, we had split the acreage for our new home from the total listing for the Inn. This was a 17 acre piece divided from the main acreage by the stream bed that ran from the road down to the river.

This was an attractive piece of land with a flat, gently sloping section for placement of a house. Behind the house location was a section of trees running down a steep slope to a flat hay field, and then down another steep slope to the Rock River. Over time, my plan envisioned use of the nine acre hay field as a golf driving range and three Par 3 golf greens for personal use.

Life became even more active as we began showing the Inn and property to prospective buyers. At the same time, the Inn was still open for Inn business, and requiring our attention to all the details of running the Inn. Winter had passed, and the activity of setting cross country ski trails was no longer a factor. It was time for haying, so there was a lot of activity for the two weeks that normally spanned. I was the principal worker in haying, but Sandra was also actively involved on the days of picking up hay bales from the field and loading them into the barn.

While the early marketing activity for the Inn was kicking off, we had to overlap our Inn business with decisions on the type of house we wanted to build. We had heard of a very good architect/contractor team, Williams and Frehsee, and it didn't take long to decide on them. The house design we selected was to be built on a post and beam concept, and I spent time with the team's architect, Jim Williams, laying out the floor plan. The company, the team suggested, would provide all the materials including individual posts, beams, and other building materials ready for erecting the home. All of the materials were specially milled and coded so that the home could be constructed by following the alphabet and numbers of the fully planned sequence for the basic house frame. In addition to all the framing, the materials they supplied included cedar clapboard siding, cedar shake roofing shingles, windows and doors.

The plan was for me to become the general contractor. I selected Jim Williams and Dennis Frehsee to erect the building and proceed to closing it in. I would select the other sub-contractors to carry it to completion.

Sandra's 57th birthday was very special. I had arranged for delivery of all the building materials on her birthday, and on that day the trucks pulled up with a very large banner reading HAPPY BIRTHDAY SANDRA. All of the basic construction materials were stacked next to the basement and first floor decking already constructed. Williams and Frehsee then went to work to erect the house, so that it was totally closed in and air tight by Christmas. My description of this process should not be interpreted as a simple job. The timbers, for the most part, were large and required brute force to be put in place. The crew worked through the month of December in conditions that were mostly snow-free, but with temperatures that kept below freezing for the entire month. The barrel that I loaded with wood and kept burning was a popular place for hand warming.

My plan was to hold off on completion of the house until we had a sale of the Inn. I borrowed a wood stove to keep the house heated over the rest of the winter, and would go over every day, making sure the wood stove was stocked with fire wood and doing its job of heating. The house was designed to be very energy efficient, and was very economical to heat.

When we had the signed Inn purchase contract in hand, I initiated some interior construction that would make the house livable for us. This would allow us to move in when the sale of the Inn closed, and we would live there while the house was being finished, literally under our feet. That was in June, and by October we had a party for the construction crews that had helped us build this rather impressive home.

In retrospect, we had overbuilt the home. The two of us had no real need for the size and some of the special features, but for the five years we lived there it was living pleasure. I have talked about the cold of Vermont, but the floor radiant heating allowed us to be barefoot and toasty warm. We had wished to have comfortable places to sit and read. As a result, a library and a separate inglenook with a woodstove were created. A picture window wall offered views down to the fields below. The kitchen had all the features one could want as well as a large island with a granite top for food preparation. The kitchen had a window with a view across another field that allowed us to see the stream bed bordering our property and the barn. This became important in another part of our story that I will bring in later.

We had a large deck that wrapped around two walls on the back of the house. The local building supply company had suggested white cedar as the decking material which was a good choice. As this wood aged, it maintained a soft gray appearance which was a good match for the gray stained house siding. To avoid a common problem with decks I eliminated one strip of decking along the house and installed a steel grate in its place, along the drip line. This permitted the rain that would fall off the roof to pass through the grating and eliminate the splash back, that would have created potential rot problems over time.

I should point out that we were able to stain the siding for the entire house prior to nailing to the walls. Another nearby building supply company had a facility that stained siding by using a rather simple conveyor arrangement. I had all the siding delivered to them.

They then placed the individual clapboards on a conveyor belt that moved the boards through a spray painting station. After suitable drying times they were able to give the exterior exposure a second coat, and one coat for the side that would be placed against the house for nailing. This would give the house siding extra durability.

The house had an enclosed porch off the great room with a sliding door the same level as the deck. This was the same approach I had used at the Inn. The porch had screens during mild weather, and replacement storm windows for installation during the winter. This porch was a favorite spot for Sandra as she could hang her clothes to dry after laundry.

After living in this house over a two year period, we determined we would sell the remaining property we still owned to produce income. This consisted of the barn, pond and 52 acres. We, of course, had the contractual arrangement with the owners of our former Inn whereby they had the right of first refusal. After I explained our intent, they declined to exercise the "right" so I developed the plan.

We wanted to have minimal impact, so I decided to subdivide this 52 acre piece into two sections. One would be 15 acres and would be placed toward the far end of the property away from the barn. The natural placement for a home there would not be seen from the road. The remaining 37 acres would include the barn and pond as well as the open agricultural land. This had minimal impact on the view from the road and the former Inn across the road. I employed a septic system engineer to test and prepare septic system designs for both properties, and to pay for the designs as an additional attraction for prospective buyers

In order to do this subdivision, I had to go back through ACT 250. This then involved two State Agencies that had not been a factor in my prior 250 engagements. The first one had to do with environmental concerns. I was at the barn, when a pickup truck drove in the driveway. I asked if I could help him, and he said no and walked away along the stream bed toward the river. That was the end of visits from that agency, and then I received a written report and restrictions. There would be no development or use permitted within 50 feet of either side of the stream bed from the road down to and along the river. This restriction, if kept in place, would totally change the use of the property. It would deny use of the existing driveway from the road into the barn, and cut off access to the road into the fields.

We hired our attorney to object to the restriction. After more delaying time, the requirement was rescinded, but the Department of Agriculture then became involved. One of their missions is to maintain Vermont's position as an agricultural State and the concern was that the potential development intrudes on the agricultural use of the fields. I did have a visit from the Vermont Secretary of Agriculture's office. Unlike the prior visit about the stream bed, this was a polite and cordial exchange as we walked in the field. I was able to satisfactorily explain the subdivision and the sites of two homes without impact on the agricultural fields. While these were resolved without canceling my plans, it is indicative of the lengths to which the State will go to control development.

This all took time, and finally when the 250 Commission scheduled their site visit, winter had come and snow had fallen. I received a telephone call to schedule the visit. At the appointed time, two cars pulled into the barn driveway and the Commissioners stepped out without boots, and one in high heels. The snow was deep, and the part of the land development they wanted to see was nearly 1,000 feet away with no trail or driveway. We stood at the barn and talked. One of them had stepped in the barn, complimented it, and said that since it was a historic structure, no development could be done affecting the barn.

Finally, the development request was approved, and I could proceed. The sale of the smaller 15 acre piece occurred within two months. The larger piece including the barn and pond was sold but took another six months. A part of my deal in selling was that I would pay for the development of a shared driveway accessing the two homes to be constructed. My last direct involvement with this property was completion of the driveway from the road to their home sites.

Barn and Horses

The thought of any extensive renovation of the barn had never been seriously in our mind when we had originally considered buying the property. Neither of us had ever done much with horses in our growing-up years. I think we realized there would be some routine maintenance of the barn, and of course, the aspect of haying had been drawn to our attention.

This is how it happened.

First, this was a classic barn; big and good looking; a barn anyone would be proud of having. The high gambrel roof and silo gave it a substantial appearance and a style that, the more we looked at it, seemed to talk to us as if to say: "*if you are going to have a country inn you will have to include me in your plans.*" The silo was the first element to draw my attention. Upon examination, it had an obvious weakness. The base of it had developed some rot and there was some tipping, not unlike the Leaning Tower of Pisa, but not as severe. When I had been in the service in the US Marines, I had been on military cruise duty in the Mediterranean where I visited Pisa and climbed the tower.

This experience may have given me enough sensitivity to encourage me to undertake some silo repair. I was able to construct some vertical support timbers inside the base of the silo and also to add interior horizontal ties that would strengthen it. This work was hidden from the outside view and added some years to the continued life of the silo. Having started that, the next easy work was getting rid of the metal stanchions that were still in place in the barn from its last 1940's days of dairy farming. These stanchions were no longer needed as we definitely had no thoughts of reestablishing a dairy farm.

Our major renovation effort began with the house and our concentration stayed there. As our life was changing, we became very lucky in that our daughter Laurie's life was changing also. Nearly a year and a half after we had made our move to Vermont, Laurie moved back from Seattle to spend some time with us, and was able to give us a hand with some of our projects. She had made local contact with a woman from the area that owned horses, and who had expressed interest in boarding them in our barn. This woman's longer term plan was to breed thoroughbred horses with her special stallion. Laurie passed on this idea to us, and the idea of horses adding further to the scenic, bucolic nature of our Inn was intriguing. Also, the idea of income from the boarding was appealing.

We thought more about the idea of the horses and decided that since the barn was across the road, we could keep barn renovation expenses separate from any of the work we were going to do in preparing the Inn. In speaking with Shel, our tax advisor, we learned we could keep separate books on the barn and the Inn and report our farm income and expenses separately. In addition to the horses we would have income from haying. The woman had only the stallion and two mares so they wouldn't add a need to build additional stall space in the barn. And, of course, she did need a place for these horses, and with our naturally compassionate natures, we would be doing a kind thing. We overlooked the old story that some of our readers may be aware of: what happens when the camel gets his nose inside the tent? Over time he takes up all the room in the tent and the tent becomes his. Well, that is what gradually happened.

Our experience with the horses was entirely new for us. We had horses using the barn and fields for several years, but we never had ownership during that period. Nor did we tie them into any operation of the Inn. We had been advised, that the need for, and cost of, insurance would never justify including horses for guests, so we never attempted anything more than boarding. We always treated the horses as "pretty to look at", and you will see that we improved the barn and fields in keeping with that concept. Guests always understood there would be no activity with the horses beyond watching. The woman who owned the horses was very appreciative of our improvements in the stables and fencing on the fields.

The barn stables were built in two stages. The first stage came after Sandra and I had moved to England on our two year assignment. By this time, Laurie had decided to stay permanently in Vermont and live at our Inn, so she would supervise construction while we were gone. The horse lady had asked if she could add some horses to those she already had. We agreed, knowing that we would have to add some stalls.

First, we strengthened the fence in the barnyard between the barn and the pond, then modified the barn with a ramp so the stallion could come directly from his corner stall out into his barnyard. Naturally, the mares would need a fenced-in pasture so this new fencing came next. As might be expected, the stallion performed his job of breeding with the mares, and there were new foals that added a wonderful new touch to the scenic picture. At this point, the new pasture was adequate in size.

The former dairy cow stanchions had been removed and the space would be perfect to convert to horse stalls for the big stallion and five other horses. The stallion would have his stall with the separate door and improvement of the ramp for him to go out to the barnyard whenever he wished. This would require new fencing for the barnyard. The new barnyard would fence out the pond and would require a new water source for the barn. When this was a dairy farm, there was no fence between the barn and pond so it was available for water for the cows.

Having had good luck with the well drilling across the road at the Inn, we made arrangements for Amon to manage the barn well drilling operation. Laurie successfully managed the barn project of new horse stalls as well as overseeing the continuing work in the Inn. She and Ed personally built the fence around the barnyard. An interesting aspect of this is that it was done after snow had fallen and the ground had been covered for some time. Earlier in this story, you were told about the freezing zone under the ground; but one of the unique characteristics of nature is that snow can also serve as an insulator. Enough snow had fallen earlier, so that snow in the barnyard had kept the ground from freezing. Laurie and Ed were able to dig the post holes by hand and complete the fence.

After we returned from England and finished the work to open the Inn we found the horse situation was continuing to change. The stallion kept on doing what stallions do, and the horse population was increasing. There was an advantage to more horses; they ate the hay we had been growing, and the income from that was being added to the boarding fees for the increasing number of horses. This had the potential of a reasonable income.

After some more discussion, I agreed to do some additional reconstruction work on the interior of the barn as well as build more fences for horse pastures. I asked Bill, our carpenter, to come back. He, Darren, and I set to work in the barn. We first completed the construction of the barn's second floor. This had been open over about 25% of the entire first floor. We built floor joists and floored in the entire area except for an 8 foot by 8 foot space that we kept open for throwing down hay. These new floor joists helped to strengthen the front wall which had originally been in danger of collapsing. We also took out the difficult–to-climb ladder and built a stairway that made it easier to access the upper floor. We then built additional stalls on the front wall for the increased number of horses.

With the increasing number of horses, we needed more fenced-in pasture for grazing. Darren and I started building fencing, and by the time we were done we had added about five acres of horse pasture. Digging post holes in our rocky Vermont soil is not an easy job. We found that the post hole digging attachment I mounted on my tractor wouldn't work very well. My solution was to go for overkill. I mounted my backhoe on the tractor and dug post holes with that. The holes were too large but were much easier to dig. Darren would place the posts in the hole, then we would backfill the dirt. This did the job, and the end result was a success.

When all of this was done, we had an outstanding arrangement for horses. We had one experience in the field that was quite dear. Normally, the mares would have their foals in the barn. One of the foals, though, was born in the field at the most distant point from the barn. Also, normally, a new foal manages to gain its footing on all four legs by itself. This foal in the field, for some reason unknown to me or its owner, was having difficulty in standing and its mother couldn't seem to understand it either. The owner thought we should get the foal into the barn so I volunteered to carry the foal in my arms. This was a unique sight as I labored across the field with this young foal in my arms covered by a blanket, and its mother walking close behind me with her head over my shoulder. I placed the foal into the foaling stall in the barn where, after some effort, she was able to stand. The owner was very happy and the mother appeared pleased also. The foal did develop into a good, strong horse.

We had horses over a five year period, beginning with three and increasing to the final count of fourteen. Our boarding agreement covered the barn stalls, pastures and hay for their food. The owner also supplemented their hay with grain, but she bought that from local suppliers separate from the agreement I had. The owner had become seriously in arrears in our bill, as well as the grain suppliers, and it became obvious that our chances of being paid were extremely low. After a long period, amounting to an unpaid bill of nearly twenty thousand dollars, under terms of the agreement, I took control of two of the mature horses. We quickly sold one, and donated the other to a private school for their riding program.

It was with a combination of sorrow and relief that I evicted the owner with her remaining horses, but we were compensated for this by our life with the creatures we called Hansel and Gretel.

In our last year of the horses we had begun living a story that we called "*Free To Fly.*" I do not believe the memoir of our life creating this country inn could be complete without including the story of the two creatures we affectionately called Hansel and Gretel. Both Sandra and I were fortunate to become involved in the rescue of these wild creatures who began to live in our pond, and were with us over a nearly three year period.

This is based on the true story from notes written by Sandra over their life with us. The first creature, a Mallard duck, who was rescued at a young age from what was destined to be his reluctant place of honor on a dinner table and took up residence on our pond. The second wild creature, a Snow goose, was separated from her migrating flock. She landed in the same pond with the mallard, where they became fast friends and soul mates. The duck's wings had been clipped before he was rescued making it impossible for him to fly. The snow goose was always free to fly, but this improbable bonding compelled her to be a vital part of the duck's life.

* * *

The story of these two creatures, excerpted from my 2015 published book <u>Free To Fly</u>, is included in the following pages of this memoir. There are episodes of joy and tragedy as we share their life together. You will see them settle into their pond home and how we help them find the necessary housing to survive harsh Vermont winters. This is a story of joy, tragedy, anxiety, homecoming, interaction with other animals, poignant goodbyes, and most of all, dedication.

Free To Fly
WILLIAM CASSILL

The Rescue

As our story begins, it is in the late spring and we can look down from our vantage point at the inn at the lovely scene of barn, pond, willow trees, and pastures with grazing horses. Beyond are the fields just ready for a late spring haying.

Sandra was working in the inn preparing for the guests that were expected later in the day when she received a phone call from a friend in the village telling her some young Mallard ducks had escaped from someone's duck pen and were in her yard. "Perhaps you can catch them and take them to your pond, because I don't have any place for them here."

"Can't they just fly off" Sandra asked.

"No, their young wings have apparently been clipped. The trailing feathers along the wings' outer edges had been plucked or trimmed back, so no matter how hard they flapped, they could not create enough lift to fly. Their owner was either keeping them to be sold as pets, or to end up on the dinner table."

Sandra said reassuringly, " I'll be down in a few minutes with my son-in-law, Darren. Bill is away in town. We'll get some boxes and some corn so we can attract them."

They drove to the friend's house and spent quite a bit of time trying to catch the ducks who were more interested in evasion and scurrying around. Finally they were successful in trapping two of them, but the third was able to escape into the nearby woods. As they returned to the pond, they released them into the friendly water where they very quickly swam off to the center. The remaining corn was then spread on the ground at the edge of the pond where the ducks, sensing they were not going to be bothered, began their eating.

This became a daily routine as Bill or Sandra spread corn on the banks of the pond, and the ducks soon accepted this as their home. With their new home and all the food they wanted, the two ducks showed no interest in flying or concern about their handicap. As summer passed, the ducks grew into handsome Mallard males, with beautiful green heads, necks ringed in white, chestnut-colored breasts and gray backs.

As Vermont moves from summer into fall, the days begin to change from sunny and warm to sunny and crisp, the kind of day where you want to wear a jacket in the early mornings and evenings. But the middle of the day is comfortable enough to shed your jacket. These are the days when the color of Vermont changes and each day gives the feeling of being in a special place. These are also the days when you can look into the fresh blue sky and see flocks of migrating birds as they fly overhead headed south for their winter homes. But these are also the days when we humans must also begin preparing for the long winter ahead.

It was near the end of one of these days, when Bill was out in the fields doing some clean-up work on his tractor, that he looked up and saw a goose beginning to circle lower over his fields. “That is strange” he thought. “That goose is by itself, and normally they would be with a large flock”. As he was observing, the goose disappeared behind a grove of trees toward the other end of his fields. “Well, I think I better forget about the goose and get back to the barn before it gets dark,” he thought, and turned his tractor for the barn.

That night after Sandra had prepared and served dinner for the inn guests, Bill told her of his experience with the goose. The two of them were puzzled as it seemed strange to see a single goose. As Bill described what he saw, they both thought it could have been a Snow goose.

Bill said, “You know, Sandra, I recall reading that the Snow goose is quite different than what people normally visualize when you say goose. For most it evokes an image of the Canada goose - they are rather large and in many communities are those you see walking around ponds, making noise and generally fouling the grounds."

Sandra pulled out her encyclopedia, found Snow Goose and read, *"pure white, have black feathers at the tips of their wings giving appearance of black edging, graceful in flight, smaller, more delicate than Canada geese"*, and it goes on to say *"they mate for life and have been known to serve as a kind of watch dog if they are in with other animals"*.

"Well," Bill said, "I don't know where she went, but let's hope a fox or coyote doesn't find her."

"I know," Sandra said, "sometimes I worry that our two ducks could have that problem, but then I realize they have the pond to keep them safe. Well, shall we finish cleaning up here and prepare for our guests tomorrow morning. They are going to be leaving after breakfast."

Escape and Arrival

The next morning, after the heavy activity of providing breakfast for the full house of guests, and saying goodbyes, the Inn quieted down. Bill and Sandra stepped out on the front porch to take a few breaths of the fresh fall air before proceeding on with the many chores. As they were standing there, Bill said, "Look, Sandra, is that a fox out there in the lower field?"

Sandra looked very carefully and said, "I think you're right. What are you going to do? I have heard enough about the possibility of rabies that I don't like having them around."

"I'll get my rifle from our gun rack and scare him away," Bill said as he went to the rack and unlocked it. He went out the door, down past the barn and proceeded slowly into the field. As he walked, he thought, "That fox must be stalking something. I better be quiet. I need to get as close as possible if I'm going to hit him with this .22 rifle. I should target practice more often because I'm a poor shot."

As he moved across the field, he could see the fox moving very slowly, intent on whatever he was stalking. The ground had enough little hills and depressions that Bill couldn't see what the fox was after. He thought to himself, "All these hills and depressions are the work of those pesky woodchucks that love to eat our hay as it grows. If I could ever get rid of them, we would have more hay for the horses. Well, I'll think about that another time and pay attention or the fox will hear me."

At that moment, something made the fox look around, spot Bill and immediately started running away. They can be very fast and this one sure was. Bill tried a shot but had no chance of hitting him. With the noise of the rifle, a goose suddenly flew into the air and headed down toward the end of the fields.

"Wow, that was close," Bill thought, "that fox came so close to getting her. I wonder where she will go now. Well, the fox is scared and won't stick around here so I'll go back up to the Inn to see what I can do around there."

* * *

The next morning, Sandra arose early and, as usual, looked out to see if the ducks were in the pond and swimming around near the edge as they usually did while they waited for her to bring down their corn. To her surprise, there was something else in the pond. Across the pond from the two ducks was a white goose apparently not sure if it could join in with the two ducks. The ducks also seemed cautious about this newcomer.

Bill was just coming down the stairs when Sandra excitedly cried out to him, "Come look at our pond! The Snow goose must have flown into the water sometime last evening! This is exciting!!"

Bill and Sandra decided they should stay away from the pond, as they were concerned they might chase the goose away. They felt there could be something wrong with the goose since she would normally have a mate with her and would be part of a large migrating flock. Perhaps she had been injured and was unable to keep up with her flock and had possibly lost her mate. In any case, they felt she should be given some time and space to see what she would do with the ducks.

They looked at the pond from the inn windows several times during the day and saw that the three of them were beginning to move closer together. They agreed the next morning might be a good time to approach the pond. They needed to provide food for the ducks and hopefully the goose would join in.

* * *

The next morning Bill and Sandra looked out at the pond and saw that the three of them were fairly close together, the ducks swimming practically shoulder to shoulder and the goose swimming independently. As Bill and Sandra slowly approached the pond, the ducks began swimming over to the edge where their corn would be tossed on the ground. They always waited until the corn was on the ground at the edge of the pond and their humans had walked away before waddling on the ground to the corn. The goose remained out at the center of the pond just watching what was going on.

This procedure of the goose in the center and the feeding of the ducks lasted about a week before the goose and ducks apparently felt comfortable enough to operate as a group. Thereafter, they ate together.

Tragedy Strikes

Meanwhile, during the week several things happened. The pond was beginning to ice with a thin, narrow band around the edge. This icing would continue slowly over the next few weeks as winter began to set in until it would become an ice-covered pond. It had become obvious to Bill and Sandra, that these three had become close friends and would stay together over the winter unless the Snow goose found a reason to fly off.

Sandra called the Vermont Department of Wildlife to explain that a wild Snow goose had landed in our pond. She had heard from friends in the village that a flock of Snow geese had recently stopped at a river about five miles away. She asked the Wildlife Agent who answered the phone if there was any way to get the Snow goose to join with this flock before they left the area on their way south. Sandra explained that she was concerned that when the pond was fully iced we would need to move the ducks to a shelter for the winter, and she was concerned about what we should do for the Snow goose. Could we possibly keep it in the same cage?

The agent explained that it is against the wildlife laws to imprison a wild creature, but she would ask others in her department what they thought should be done, and she would call Sandra.

The next day, the agent called, saying she had talked to two other biologists who said that if the goose wanted to, she would fly to join the other flock. She explained that it normally requires a special license to cage a wild creature, and this takes a long time. But, what we were considering doing sounded like a compassionate thing to do. Sandra also asked about birds' diet and was told the best diet was a mixture of cracked corn, laying pellets and whole corn which Sandra bought on her next trip to market.

Later that week tragedy struck. One night, for no understandable reason, one of the male ducks swam under the iced part of the pond and apparently got trapped. The next morning Darren saw there were only two at the pond – a duck and the goose. His first thought was "maybe a fox or coyote got the missing Mallard," but as he looked around, he could see no trace of feathers which would have been a sure sign of some deadly act. As he was puzzling about the mystery, he looked carefully at the ice and remaining clear water and found the outline of the duck's body under the ice.

Darren was able to fish him out and brought him up to the Inn for a proper funeral. Fortunately, the weather had not yet been cold enough to freeze the ground so a grave could be dug for his final resting place.

He lies in a high place overlooking the Inn and lower fields next to the beloved Inn cat named Tiger. Tiger had passed on at age seventeen after a very comfortable life including traveling and living with Bill, Sandra and their family in France.

The Bonding Begins

This then left the remaining male Mallard and female Snow goose together in the pond, and thus began the time that bound them into a nearly inseparable couple. Before the accident, the three of them had formed as a group swimming together and when the grain had been placed on the bank of the pond they would be up eating together. Now that there were just the two of them they seemed to become even closer. As the ice was forming they no longer had as much water to swim in, but it became obvious that the Snow goose began to assume a protective role.

Perhaps, the natural "guard dog" role that Snow geese have been known for doesn't apply only to the barnyard situations that have been written about them. When they were in the water she began placing herself between the Mallard and the edge of the pond. Whenever Bill or Sandra or any of the inn guests would walk down to the pond, we would see many examples of this instinct over the coming years of their time together. Normally, it was the goose being protector, but on occasion we would see their roles reversed as the duck took over.

While this close companionship was developing, Wimble, the inn dog, began to spend more time around the pond. The Mallard and Snow goose were, of course, not sure what to make of this and chose to keep their distance out in the water. This is the time to re-introduce Wimble; a Bernese Mountain Dog who was very big and friendly without a mean or excitable bone in his body. He was now one and a half years old, and was bright and very well trained. He was respectful and always immediately responded to commands. Bill and Sandra were sure that he wanted to make friends, but to the duck and goose he was a threat, and they kept the greatest possible distance between them.

Over time, this began to change. Wimble normally spent most of his time trailing after Bill except when Bill was on the tractor and then Wimble would go watch over his friends in the pond. Eventually he began to go in the pond and stand arm pit deep watching them. The duck and goose would float a little closer but they would never put themselves dangerously near. The goose would inevitably assume the protector role by being the closest to Wimble.

Sandra and Bill would observe this interaction and they were sure that Wimble must be thinking to himself, "I only want to get close to them to show I just want to be their friend."

The Winter Home

As the ice continued to slowly close in, Sandra was concerned and said to Bill, "We really need to provide some housing for them. They won't be able to stay there much longer. And when the pond freezes solid, our duck will be in real trouble. The goose can fly, but he will be easy prey for the fox."

"I know," agreed Bill, "I have been thinking about a solution. I know where to get a chain link fence with a gate and a dog house. I think Darren and I can set up the fencing as an enclosure up against the corral fence of the barn on the pond side, and we can put a dog house inside so they can get out of the weather. They will also have enough space outside the dog house and inside the fence for some exercise. We can put a tarpaulin over the top of the enclosure to keep a lot of the snow off. I believe this would be a good home for them. What do you think?"

"I think that is a great answer! And I have an idea how we can get them from the pond to their new home. We can begin spreading a trail of their food from the pond toward the enclosure, making the trail longer each time until they are comfortable and reach the gate. We can then close them in."

"You know" she said excitedly, "this is like Hansel and Gretel with their trail of bread! Let's name them. The Mallard will be Hansel and the Snow goose will be Gretel.

Bill and Darren began the task of erecting the enclosure, resting the back wall against the barnyard fence and within two days had it all set up with the tarpaulin over the top for protection. While all this activity was going on, the stallion would come out of his stall in the barn and stand with his head over the fence to watch what was going on. This was of real interest to him and he became a steady viewer of Hansel and Gretel's activities.

And so over the next several days, Bill or Sandra placed their corn in a trail that when complete would make its way from the pond edge to the enclosure and into the dog house. Each day the trail of corn would become a little longer so that Hansel and Gretel would not be frightened, and after four days Bill was able to carefully close the gate behind them while they were eating the corn in the enclosure.

"Now, Bill said, "they are safe for the long winter but the only thing remaining is fresh water. How will we provide that?"

Sandra's immediate response was "I'll bring them fresh water every day in a pail from the Inn"

"Sandra, I know you mean that, but you know that is a long walk from the Inn down the road and across behind the barn out to the pond. And you know there will be a lot of snow to tramp through."

"I know that, but Hansel and Gretel give me so much pleasure that I can do that for them."

Winter of Dedication

As winter set in, with the pond fully frozen, the snow began and Hansel and Gretel were safe in their protected home. Sandra began her daily trek struggling through the snow and cold carrying their food and life-necessary water. This could have been considered hardship duty as it required Sandra trudging through the snow on a rather difficult trip from the Inn, down the road to the barn and beyond and along the barnyard fence to the enclosure. This sounds difficult, and it was, but it was one of the highlights of her day knowing how vital it was for these creatures.

From the time they were in their new home, it took several days before they would use the dog house, but from then on they would use it at night. As Sandra would arrive in the morning, she would be accompanied by Wimble. As they arrived, Hansel and Gretel would exit their house ready for food and water. As Sandra would talk to them, Gretel showed real interest by stretching out her neck and cocking her head. Meanwhile Wimble would stand there watching them, and while it seemed clear Hansel and Gretel would never become his buddies, they all appeared to be somewhat comfortable with the short distance between them.

As they became accustomed to the routine of being in their enclosure, the roles of Hansel and Gretel seemed to reverse themselves. When the two of them had been in the pond or up on the bank, Gretel had assumed the role of protector. She always inserted herself between Hansel and whoever came to the pond. Now, since they were in the enclosure, Hansel became the one who would take the lead and serve as protector. He would be the first one out of their little house and always maneuvered himself between the goose and any visitors. Gretel seemed to accept this.

As we watched from the warmth of the inn, we could see Sandra's dedication while she trudged through the starkness of the winter landscape. The scene portrayed the giant willow trees devoid of leaves. The pond on some days was deep with snow and on others the wind whipped the snow into drifts leaving the pond interspersed with bare ice spots. The skies would be a dark gray with the promise of more snow and other days the sky would be bright blue. The snow covered fields would have cross-country skiers enjoying the flat hay fields before they moved in to the trees and challenging slopes of the hillside.

And so go the long winter months!

Excitement of Spring

Spring is a wonderful time in Vermont. In the beginning it is barely noticeable, but then you realize the days have become just a little warmer and there is some snow melt. Then the pace of warming seems to pick up and you begin to see patches of grass. In the distance you can hear water running and you realize the river is beginning to break open. The river, which during the summer is shallow and slow moving, becomes a torrent, and for a period of time is a resource for adventurous kayakers to practice their considerable skills. In the skies, the northern migration of birds begins.

All of the signs of coming spring have an effect on Hansel and Gretel. They begin to have more movement in their enclosure and their wing flapping seems to have a quicker beat. It is almost as though they are saying, "Come on Bill and Sandra, it's time to let us out".

Even though the pond was still iced over, Sandra felt their excitement and thought they should have an outing. So on a sunny morning after she brought them their food and water she opened the gate and watched them. They immediately scampered through the gate, made a brief stop to look around and headed for the pond. As they went down the bank, they found ice but still proceeded out on the pond. It became obvious after a short time that they didn't really understand this frozen water.

Sandra saw how vulnerable they were and determined that when they were back in their enclosure they would not be let out again until the pond was free of ice. Hansel and Gretel must have realized this was not a good situation for them and slowly made their way back to their food and water. Sandra kept watch on them, and when they were back in the enclosure, she closed and latched the gate. The next morning, as Sandra came down with their food and water, they came out of their little house as they normally did seemingly content with their life.

The next days were warm and the bare ground began to get a little muddy heralding the start of the Vermont *mud season.* There are six seasons in Vermont; the normal spring, summer, fall and winter plus two others, M*ud Season and 'Taint Season. Mud season*, as we have indicated, is that time when the deep frozen earth begins to thaw and release moisture turning a good part of Vermont, especially the dirt roads, into mud. '*Taint season* is that period of time between the colorful fall foliage and before the arrival of snow for skiing. In other words, *"taint foliage and 'taint skiing.* These two seasons are not good for tourism which is so vital to the economy of Vermont.

Over the next couple of days, the signs of spring continued. The warmer weather brought the sound of river ice beginning to break up, while overhead we began hearing the noises of migrating birds. Spring was beginning and the long winter was at an end.

One morning, after the Hansel and Gretel outing, Sandra went down to their enclosure and to her great surprise found the gate standing open. Neither Hansel nor Gretel came out of their house. She stepped into the enclosure and peered in the house. Hansel was lying on the bed of hay not moving and there was no sign of Gretel. There was no sign of struggle – no feathers which would have indicated a predator. Hansel showed no obvious sign of physical injury but also no sign of interest in moving. Sandra placed the water bowl in the house for him, and closed the gate.

Returning to the inn she told Bill of what she had found. "What do you think happened, Bill? Who could have opened the gate?"

Bill replied, "Yesterday, late afternoon, there were some visitors to the barn – apparent friends of the woman who has been stabling her horses here. There were some children and possibly they were curious and opened the gate. It was nearly dark when they left so that could be the way Gretel got out."

"I am so worried about Gretel" Sandra said, "I hope she is all right and joined in with one of the migrating flocks of Snow geese. I am also so worried about Hansel. You should have seen him. He was just lying there without moving. He looked so sad and dejected. I am going back down there to see if he ate or drank anything."

Over the next three days, Hansel would not eat or drink and even when Sandra opened the gate for him he showed no interest in leaving. He seemed enormously depressed and with his head hanging low would just muck about in his enclosure pecking dejectedly in the mud. By now the pond was free of ice so Sandra left the gate open all day hoping he would go into the pond. He finally left the enclosure and made his way slowly into the water and began swimming around. He returned to his normal eating habits with the corn placed on the bank of the pond, but he looked lonely without his friend, Gretel.

The Return

And then, a big surprise!

Two weeks from the day Gretel left, Sandra looked out the inn window and called excitedly to Bill, “Come see this, Gretel is back.” Down in the pond they could see her swimming alongside Hansel as though she had never been gone. Sandra immediately went down to the pond with their food and they came right up to her. Their life had now returned to normalcy.

Over the next several days, it appeared to Bill and Sandra as though Gretel was trying to convince Hansel that he should begin to fly and join in on her flying excursions. The two of them would be in the water at the edge of the pond and Gretel would take off flying across while Hansel watched. The distance across the pond is about 150 feet, and as Gretel would reach the opposite side she would do a graceful U-turn and settle down in the water. She would then flap her wings as though she was saying, “Come on you can do it!”

Hansel, in response, would simply flap his wings and paddle furiously toward her. Perhaps his wings having been clipped as a young duck or the weight he had put on from his supply of corn were just too much to overcome. This went on for several days and after the continuous encouragement by Gretel, he was finally able to become airborne. But the maximum distance Bill or Sandra ever saw him achieve was perhaps eight to ten feet before landing back in the water with a splash followed by swimming over to her side.

Bill and Sandra speculated many times on the experiences Gretel might have had. Perhaps the time the gate had been left open some migrating snow geese might have landed in the pond that night and encouraged her to join them. Perhaps the sounds of migrations overhead attracted her and she gave into her natural instincts. The length of time she was gone could have led her into any combination of experiences. Whatever the reasons might be and experiences she may have had, the one sure thing is, *her personal bond with Hansel was so strong that it overcame all else.*

Search for Solitude

As spring turned into summer, life in the pond turned into the normal routines with Hansel and Gretel swimming around and enjoying their life. Occasionally Bill and Sandra would see other water fowl arrive at the pond, and if they showed any interest in staying, Hansel would become aggressive. Perhaps he was concerned they might entice Gretel to fly away with them and he would rapidly pursue them. After they would fly away, he would turn and swim back to Gretel who sat bobbing in the water waiting for him.

That summer, the pond was becoming over-populated with frogs so Bill arranged with a young neighborhood boy to catch frogs and place them in a large five- gallon bucket. The boy was excited with the prospect of earning five cents for each small frog and ten cents for large frogs. Bill's plan was to drive the bucket of frogs to a pond nearly two miles away and release them to a new home.

The day of the frog catching was a bright, sunny day with a promise of a high temperature – a perfect day to be in the pond's cool water for swimming and earning money. The boy had arranged for two of his friends to help, and they were accompanied by two mothers who brought a picnic lunch. The picnic table in the shade of one of the massive willow trees was perfect for the mothers.

The boys immediately set about their job with enthusiasm. They had brought with them a long handled net that they used with great skill to capture the frogs. As they placed them in the bucket, the boys would eagerly shout out the sizes:

"Large"!

"Small!!!

The bucket began to fill up and the enthusiastic sounds of laughter with shouts of "large" and "small" filled the air. The occasional shouts of "Hey, Mom, look at the size of this one" added to the joyous atmosphere.

The noises and activity were far different than the normal peaceful pond Hansel and Gretel were accustomed to. Evidently disturbed by the commotion they decided to head for another pond on the inn property.

They had never done this before, but Gretel was apparently aware of this pond from her earlier flights, so she led the way along the ground with Hansel following. They made their way from the pond up the hill on the narrow path to the narrow two lane road and began walking single file down the center of the road. They were headed for a small, shallow and peaceful pond on the other side of the road just up from the Inn.

It was at this point that Sandra saw them. As she did, she realized where they were headed. At that same instant, she saw a truck driving down the road straight for this strange sight. She quickly ran and stood in the center of the road with her hand up. The truck stopped and Sandra began to explain the situation to the driver who had seen the unexpected sight of the goose and duck. He was then very willing to wait until they were safely off the road.

At this point Hansel and Gretel apparently decided this was too much and turned in their tracks, headed back on the road and down the hill to their pond. The mothers and children considerately collected their belongings and prepared to leave so Hansel and Gretel could have their pond in peace.

By this time, the boys had filled the bucket. They gave Bill their count of large and small frogs and happily accepted their payment. The bucket was placed in Bill's truck and he drove off to the pond that would be their new home. As he left, Hansel and Gretel slipped into their water with its peaceful serenity.

The Request

A significant change occurred this summer. The horses that had occupied the barn, barnyard and fenced pastures for several years were moved away. While this did change the bucolic view from the Inn, the reduction in work effort without the horses did make it easier for Bill.

Shortly after the horses left, Bill received a telephone call from a local acquaintance who asked for help for his family. The family lived outside of the nearby village up in the hills in a home that could easily be considered as a kind of an *Old McDonald's F*arm. They had a small barn with fenced in areas that housed a number of different animals including a horse, a cow, goats, sheep, chickens and turkeys. They had developed this as a means of building discipline and responsibility in their children who raised the animals in a 4H Club program in the local schools.

He sounded desperate as he explained their situation. Their oldest goat, and most importantly, a long-time family pet, had recently given birth. The experience had so exhausted the old nanny goat that she died. He went on to say that these Vermont soils are so hard and rocky that he didn't know how they were going to be able to dig her grave. They had already checked with local excavation contractors, but the job was so small for their large equipment that they wouldn't help them. His request of Bill was to have him come up to their farm with his tractor and back hoe to bury their pet.

Bill agreed he would drive over on his tractor and help them. The next day he attached his back hoe to his tractor and traveled the back roads to their farm in the trees. The family had been so attached to the nanny goat that they couldn't bear to watch as he began the task of burial. Without a back hoe it would have been impossible for them to dig a grave in the demanding Vermont rocky soil so Bill completely understood their situation.

After the burial was complete Bill accepted their offer of a tour of their farm. The first thing he saw was the baby goat, or kid, being bottle fed by the wife as she held him between her legs. Bill was very encouraged by that as he had wondered how the baby would survive without his mother. Continuing the tour, Bill saw two more kids, a male and a female, that had been born at about the same time to a healthy mother. He was also rather taken with their cow; she was nearly fully grown but still young and followed him around on his farm tour like a big puppy dog. As Bill met all the other animals he was very pleased with the care shown by the man and the wife. As Bill left on his tractor, they thanked him over and over for his kindness.

The next day Bill received a phone call from the wife with an unexpected offer. She explained that she and her husband had been discussing recently that they should be cutting down on the number of animals in order to reduce their work effort. And she wondered if Bill and Sandra might want to accept the three kids as a gift in thanks for the very kind burial service. This would only take place after the orphan was weaned from his bottle and the two other kids had been weaned from their mother.

Bill talked to Sandra about the offer and they both agreed this was a splendid offer. They both knew that kids could be extremely playful and agreed they would add a nice touch to the barn scene. Also they could be counted on to keep the grass and weeds chewed down in the barnyard that had previously been used by the stallion.

“That’s settled,” said Sandra, “What shall we call them?”

“Well!” replied Bill. We will have two boys and one girl. Let’s call them Thomas, Richard and Harriet.”

Arrival of The Goats

Over the next several weeks all was peaceful at the pond. Hansel and Gretel spent their time swimming around together seeming more and more content with their close friendship. When Bill had some spare time from his outdoor activities he enjoyed going to the pond to sit under the shade of one of the willow trees and enjoy the solitude.

Wimble was his constant companion and particularly liked to be close to Hansel and Gretel. As they sat on the grass, Gretel would occasionally come up and stand about four feet away. Wimble was very eager to go up to Gretel, but if he moved toward her she would fly the few feet into the water. Hansel was not interested in the closeness but did stay nearby just off the pond edge and in the water.

Bill and Sandra were thinking of getting the barn ready for the arrival of the goats after their weaning. The stallion's stall had a ramp that came directly from his stall down into the barnyard and with some modifications would be perfect for the goats. The size was adequate for the three goats. All it took was a change in one of the other stalls to create an accessible enclosure for hay and grain storage.

Having taken care of the barn, the new goat owners thought it would be fun to have a climbing area out in the goat yard. Thomas, Richard and Harriet were young kids and not much different than human young kids in terms of their need for playful activity. Goats are bright and very curious. When they encounter anything new in their environment they will investigate it. If there is a gate with a latch, unless it is very secure, they will work at it until they can open it.

They will climb on anything left in their area. On one occasion, Bill had his truck in the barnyard unloading some hay and left it for a few minutes. When he came back, Thomas was standing up on the hood surveying the barnyard. Also, the story about goats eating anything is a myth; they have much greater enjoyment of good hay and grain and will avoid weeds.

Before the goats arrived, Bill worked on the play project. There were several of the original timbers in the barn that had been left over from an earlier barn renovation. These were ideal and were used to construct a climbing gym with several levels including balance bars. This was finished and standing in the middle of the goat yard waiting for the arrival of Thomas, Richard and Harriet.

From the first arrival all three of them were very friendly to Bill and Sandra and any Inn guests that came down to visit them. They also quickly took to their play gym competing with each other to see who could be the first to the highest point, and to see who could butt the others off. This would continue to be a popular activity.

Preparing For Another Winter

Summer continued and began to change into fall and the conversation turned into the need to house Hansel and Gretel for the winter. While Sandra was willing to do the same carrying of food and water as last year, Bill thought he had a better solution. It would take construction, but would make her winter task much easier and be much better for Hansel and Gretel and the kids.

Bill explained to Sandra, "We could build an attached, covered enclosure off the side of the barn inside the goat yard. This would house Hansel and Gretel and would allow them to have a heated water tub for drinking." "And, he added, "The covered enclosure would have two sides, one for the Hansel and Gretel, and the other for Thomas, Richard and Harriet.

"That is a brilliant idea, Bill. We can use a hose from the barn sink to clean and change their water. But can we get them into their new home? The trail of corn will have to be more than twice as long."

"I think we can do it", Bill replied.

With that, Bill, along with Darren, began building the new winter home. They attached a roof to the side of the barn so that it sloped to carry off the rain and snow. Hansel and Gretel's side was fully wire fenced-in with a gate that would allow humans to enter with a latch to keep it closed and secure from the goats.

The wall between their enclosure and the goats was wire fenced and designed with a water tub sitting underneath it on the ground so the water was shared equally on either side. A water heater designed for farm use kept the water from freezing. Thomas, Richard and

Harriet were free to eat hay or drink water from their side whenever they wished. The roof kept their hay dry.

The side for Hansel and Gretel was more elaborate. It was more like a split-level home. They had a raised platform for their sleeping area which was kept supplied with clean hay for their bedding. There was a small ramp they used to walk down from the sleeping area for their water and a ramp from that they used to get down to the ground area.

There was also a small gate at ground level that would be used for Hansel and Gretel to enter their winter home after they followed their trail of corn from the pond. The large gate was for Bill and Sandra to enter for care – food, bedding and replacement of clean water. This was the gate to be kept tightly closed and secure from the goats.

Thomas, Richard and Harriet had been having a great time involving themselves in the construction work by Bill and Darren. It was like having three children underfoot while working. There was a need to always be vigilant so that none of them could make it through an open gate and outside the goat yard. When the project was finished we had the ultimate test – could any of the goats open the gate into Hansel and Gretel's side? They all tried several times and it seemed the new winter home passed the test.

Now it was time to await winter and when we would encourage Hansel and Gretel to make the longer walk from the pond to their new home.

Excitement In The New Home

Summer passed, fall came again with all of its colorful glory, and winter began its incursion. The kids had grown although not yet to their full sizes. Hansel and Gretel had a peaceful time finishing the rest of the summer swimming around their pond without any new adventures that were memorable. Life was good!

Now as snow began to fall and the pond began to ice in, it became time to again encourage Hansel and Gretel to move into their new winter home. Sandra began laying out the trail of corn as had been done last winter, spreading it over short distances each day, but it became obvious it would not be as easy. The path from the pond to their new winter home was now nearly three times as long, and half of the distance passed through a narrow area between fences before getting to the barn enclosure.

Sandra had been concerned that Gretel particularly would not be secure in making the walk, and she was right. The two of them would go as far as the shelter they used last winter near the pond, but would not venture beyond. So a plan was decided to trail the corn into the old shelter and when they went in the gate would be closed so they could not get back to the pond. Bill and Darren would then physically carry them to the new winter home.

The next day after laying out the trail of food, Hansel and Gretel did exactly as expected and followed the trail into their old enclosure. Bill and Darren had been watching from behind the closest large Willow tree, and they went into the enclosure and closed the gate behind them. This was the first time anyone had been in their shelter with them so at first Hansel and Gretel were very nervous.

Bill and Darren remained quiet for some time to allow them to settle down. Bill then picked up Gretel and Darren picked up Hansel.

They were gentle in their handling so there wouldn't be any damage. The most secure way to hold them was to place one arm around the body and the other hand to gently encircle their neck without pressure. This would keep them from squirming loose, because if they did there would be very little chance of getting them again.

As they did this, Bill found that Gretel suddenly went limp in his arms with her head slumping down. Bill was concerned that Gretel was hurt and relaxed his hold on her neck. She immediately became very alert and tried to free herself. "Aha!" Bill said. "You were just trying the old possum play-dead trick." So he snugged her up a bit in his arms to make the trip.

Meanwhile Hansel wasn't any trouble and Bill and Darren then walked them to the new home. As they approached the enclosure, Sandra opened the small door and they were carefully eased into their new home. The three kids were overcome with curiosity and butted the fence trying to work the gate latch free. All of the careful construction work paid off and the gate remained secure.

Throughout the winter, the goats kept trying to open the gate, and when Bill or Sandra would go in with Hansel and Gretel with fresh food or to change the water they would be right there checking for ways they could be part of this. Hansel and Gretel had settled in and seemed to enjoy their new and upgraded accommodations. All winter, the goats were allowed out into the fenced-in barnyard. Now they had an additional amusement, a new gate to worry with.

Early one morning Richard was butting his head against the new gate when, to his delight, it opened. The excitement aroused Hansel and Gretel. Instinctively, as their gate swung wide, they burst out. Gretel took flight in confused desperation, skimming over the outer fence and sliding to a landing on the snow covered pond. Hansel also bolted in panic, but was not able to fly the height and distance to clear the fence. After an effort to try flying he struggled his way on the ground pushing through the snow to the fence. Gretel saw him and fluttered back to be next to him on the pond side of the fence.

That was how Bill and Sandra found them; the two of them crouched next to each other on opposite sides of the fence. "Hansel looks beat," Bill said. "I prefer not to pick them up again. "I'll lock the goats in the barn and then try to tramp a path in the snow for Hansel to walk along the fence line."

After enticing the goats into the barn with the promise of their favorite grain, their door was shut and bolted. If they had been left outside there would have been no way to solve Hansel and Gretel's problem with the three of them playing underfoot as Bill tried to manage Hansel.

Bill cleared a path for Hansel along the inside of the fence by stamping the snow down with his feet. He then dropped an encouraging trail of corn for Hansel to follow back to their enclosure. Gretel fluttered and followed him along on the outside. Thus side by side, they slowly wended their way home. "Silly duck," Gretel seemed to say as they entered their small enclosure, and she pecked at him affectionately on the head. This time it had been fully their choice to retreat and enter their cozy shelter. Bill then worked on the latch for the gate so none of the goats would be able to open it again.

The rest of winter passed peacefully, and the setting with Thomas, Richard and Harriet plus Hansel and Gretel became an appealing attraction for Inn guests. The hay fields were tracked for cross country skiing so before or after skiing, the guests would stop to observe the animals. While it was obvious that neither Hansel nor Gretel would ever become pets, it was comforting to see them somewhat relaxed in their environment.

Spring And A Natural Pull

Following what had been an exciting winter experience, spring arrived somewhat earlier this year. As in the previous year, Hansel and Gretel showed real excitement. Bill and Sandra, remembering last year, waited until the pond clearly had no more ice before agreeing it was time to let them out.

It was a beautiful sunny day when the innkeepers went down to the barn and opened the small gate that led directly from their home to the area outside the barnyard fence. They then stepped back so they would not be intruding on the path back to the pond. They observed Hansel and Gretel look around their enclosure to see the normally closed gate was open with Bill and Sandra standing a distance away. Gretel took the lead, with Hansel following, and slowly approached the gate. They paused and then stepped through to the outside. This was the small gate to the outside so they were able to walk directly to the pond so Hansel did not have to worry about flying over the barnyard fence.

It was, of course, possible for Gretel to fly to the pond but she started walking with Hansel following just as they had at the time of the frog catching. They made their way to the pond. The joy and freedom of being back in the water was obvious as they paddled around and around with Hansel frequently dipping his head in the water. After this, the only time they came out of the pond was for the food that Sandra would bring to them. Life was back to being very good as they settled into their normal routine.

Bill and Sandra were also in their normal Inn routine, and other than the time it took to feed them neither spent much time at the pond. But they would always be watching the pond from the Inn windows. Sandra was the one that first saw the new visitors land in the water and called out to Bill, "Come see! A small gaggle of Snow geese have just landed. There are five of them and it looks as though there are two adults and three younger ones." Bill quickly came to the window and saw a much different reaction than he might have expected. They stepped outside to have a closer view.

Hansel had promptly reacted to this sudden invasion of geese into his pond and maneuvered himself between Gretel and the visiting geese, squawking loudly. But Gretel just ignored him and swam directly over to the visitors. The six geese then went onto the pond's bank and gathered together as though they were having a conference. Hansel, left alone, stayed near the center of the pond with no apparent intention of joining the group.

Sandra looked out at the visiting flock as she continued her morning chores. Later in the morning, she noticed that the five visitors would occasionally fly off a short distance from the pond and then return. "I think they're inviting Gretel to come with them," she said to Bill, when he came in for lunch.

"That makes sense," he said. "Still, I somehow can't see her leaving Hansel." But in mid-afternoon, when Sandra looked out again, the Snow goose family was gone, and so was Gretel. Hansel was bobbing about alone in the pond.

"*Poor thing,*" Sandra said to herself. "*What will he do? Gretel must have had a natural instinct to join up with the other geese on their northern migration. I feel torn between the fact that Hansel will be alone and Gretel is free to fly with a natural family. He was so depressed last year when she went away that I am afraid he may have the same reaction. At least he has the pond to be in.*"

A little later, early in the afternoon, the phone rang. It was a neighbor who lived half a mile up the road in the center of the village. "A Snow goose showed up in my pond a little while ago," he said. "It could be yours. You don't usually see one all by itself."

"Please don't feed her" said Sandra. "Maybe she'll come home on her own." The neighbor said he'd keep her posted. Sandra turned to Bill. "Gretel may be on another pond up the road, all by herself. If she did go off with that Snow goose family, she might have found she was too weak to keep up. It has been a long time since she did any flying." Sandra looked out the window. "And now it's starting to rain."

Shortly before dusk, the phone rang again. It was the neighbor's wife. "Sandra," she said, "I believe it's your goose I found standing in the middle of the road in the rain. She looked kind of forlorn. So I shooed her out of the road into the rushes beside our pond and she seems snug for the night. Let's see what happens in the morning."

Bill and Sandra talked about going down to see what they were sure was Gretel, but decided they might just scare her away and they should just wait to see if Gretel's bond with Hansel was strong enough to bring her back.

As if the story were being scripted, the next morning as Sandra was walking to the pond with their food, Gretel swooped in over the meadow from the direction of the village and landed in the pond. The two of them immediately swam together and after a short period of just swimming around they went up on the bank to eat. All was well, again!

Sandra received another call. Two of the Inn guests, who were from Switzerland, were at the Inn at the time of Gretel flying off. They called from the Boston airport as they were waiting for their plane to depart to find out what had happened with Gretel. They were delighted to hear the good news. Over time, there were several guests who were so taken with the heart touching story about the two friends that they would call for updates.

Barnyard Changes

Throughout the summer Bill and Sandra began to see a change in the interaction between Hansel and Gretel and the goats, Thomas, Richard and Harriet. Perhaps it actually began in the spring after Hansel and Gretel left their winter enclosure to go back to the pond.

Shortly after they were in the pond swimming together as usual, we saw Gretel leave Hansel's side and fly over the fence into the barnyard. At first she stayed apart from the goats just watching them as they played. Over some time she gradually moved closer, not enough to be in the center of them, but enough that she showed she wasn't bothered by their running around. Meanwhile Hansel started by moving from the pond water to the bank and gradually to the fence where he stood watching the barnyard activity through the fence.

It is difficult to know just how Hansel and Gretel communicated with each other, but whatever it was Gretel knew she was needed in the pond. She would leave the goats and fly back over the fence into the water. Hansel would immediately waddle back to the water's edge and soon they would be together again, side by side. As time went on though, Gretel spent more time with the goats leaving Hansel alone at the fence.

Bill and Sandra would watch this and talk about it as they were quite concerned for Hansel, but didn't know what they could do about it. They thought that Gretel was acting the natural way of snow geese, that is, serving as a protector of the goats. They had spent the winter housed next to Hansel and Gretel and perhaps that close companionship had caused Gretel to feel the need to protect.

The natural effect of the barnyard fence was to automatically protect Gretel when she was away from the water. Hansel was very vulnerable. In his desire to be close to Gretel he would spend a lot of his time at the base of the fence. Since he couldn't fly, whenever he wanted to get back into the pond he would have to waddle and he wasn't very fast at that.

Bill and Sandra hadn't seen or heard of fox or coyotes in the immediate area over these last years, but they knew it could happen. They considered making an opening in the fence so Hansel could go in with Gretel and the goats but this wasn't practical. Such an opening would also let predators into the barnyard and/or let the goats out. After considering the alternatives they determined they would have to take the chance.

Meanwhile Bill and Sandra had added two new creatures to the barn. It is always important to have a barn cat to protect against small pests and rodents. A friend had told Sandra of a barn in the area where their cat had recently had a litter of kittens. When the kittens were old enough to wean from their mother Bill and Sandra went to visit. They particularly liked two of them and made arrangements with the owner to bring them back to the Inn barn. As with all kittens they were quite playful and got along very well with Thomas, Richard and Harriet. Cats normally are not known to be good friends with ducks and geese so mostly they would sit up on top of the fence posts and just watch what was going on.

Bill and Sandra had lived in England before coming back to open the Inn. While living there they had developed a fondness for the British royal family particularly Charles and Diana. It was only natural that the two kittens, brother and sister, became known as Charles and Diana.

A few weeks later Bill and Sandra observed that Hansel seemed to be missing. They could not see him from the Inn windows. Bill walked across the road and down the bank toward the pond. It was very quiet. Gretel didn't move from her place inside the fence facing the pond. Bill walked around the fence to the pond. On the pond side of the fence closest to where Gretel was standing, he found feathers, some rust-colored, some green, scattered between the fence and the water. There were signs of a scuffle. "Ah, thought Bill sadly, it looks like a fox found Hansel away from the water last night."

He looked some more and found the body of Hansel further around the pond. It was apparent he had struggled and tried to run away, but the fox had cut him off from the water. The fox had been too strong and his teeth too sharp for Hansel to survive. Something must have then scared the fox off so he had been unable to carry off Hansel's body.

Bill quickly returned to the Inn to tell Sandra the sad news. "Sandra, I'm so sorry to tell you."

"What happened?" Sandra exclaimed.

"It's Hansel!!! Something got him last night! He's dead."

"What about Gretel? Is she alright?'

"Yes," Bill said. She was inside the fence with the goats. She must have been very frightened. It looks as though she was next to the fence when it happened."

"Poor Hansel," said Sandra "He was safe on the water, but he must have spent too much time by the fence close to Gretel and didn't pay attention to his own safety."

They agreed they must bury Hansel and jointly agreed a good location would be next to Hansel's brother who had died under the pond ice and the Inn cat, Tiger. This was a prime location on the hill above the remains of the old cider mill overlooking the Inn and its fields and mountain in the distance. Bill brought Hansel up from the pond and he and Sandra prepared his resting place.

As they were laying Hansel to rest, Sandra gave voice to the thoughts both were having about the loss of their friend. "I wonder what Gretel will do. It certainly won't be the same for her without Hansel."

A Fond Farewell

Bill had heard of a family that wanted goats on their small farm. The father had earlier helped Bill with some land clearing and Bill knew they would give Thomas, Richard and Harriet a good home. Since Bill and Sandra had recently sold the Inn they thought the buyers may not want to have the responsibility of goats, and it would be better if they took this opportunity to keep them together.

A week later a pickup truck backed to the fence gate and a man and his son went in to round up the goats. It was a bittersweet moment as Sandra and Bill had developed a strong fondness for them, but were glad some children would be enjoying these fun animals. They also gave them the cats, Charles and Diana.

As they were all driven away, Bill and Sandra knew the barnyard would be different, and they wondered how Gretel would be affected by the change. They were also having their own thoughts on how they would personally feel.

* * *

Later that day Sandra and Bill greeted friends they had earlier invited for dinner. These were the first guests they had invited to the new home they had so recently moved into just down the road from the barn. They had sold the Inn but not the barn and its land.

These friends had not yet visited Bill and Sandra so they hadn't had the opportunity to see the overall layout of the land. Before dinner it was decided to take a walk across the fields and along the river to the swimming hole. They all, with Wimble, left the house and walked across the field to the barn and past the pond. Gretel had remained quiet all day, wandering alongside the old goat fence and drifting about on the pond. As they walked past the barn and on to the field they were greeted by an impressive sight and the most amazing experience of Bill and Sandra's time together with Gretel.

As they walked, Gretel flew toward them and as she drew closer she began making beautiful circles over their heads. The black trailing edge of her wings was especially beautiful as it was normally not obvious when she was on the ground in a resting position. All five plus Wimble and their graceful flying escort continued across the field to the river.

As they left the field to go through the trees and down the hill to the swimming hole, Gretel left them and flew back toward the barn.

After Bill, Sandra and the guests had some time just gazing at the slow running river and remembering Hansel, they turned back up the hill to begin the walk back home.

* * *

Again, amazement!

As they emerged from the trees onto the field, Gretel flew to them and landed on the ground about fifteen feet away and began walking with them. Wimble was anxious to get closer but he was easy to restrain with voice commands. On the few occasions he let his enthusiasm carry him closer, Gretel would simply flap her wings to get a few feet further away and then continue the walk. As they all came in sight of the barn, Gretel took off, did one more circle over them and flew toward the barn.

When they returned home Sandra felt a real sense that she should go visit Gretel. Knowing that she and Bill would someday be selling the barn and pond, and she would no longer be able to take care of Gretel, she decided she should not strengthen this personal attachment.

However, the next morning she awoke early and went immediately down to the pond. It was empty. No one was in the hutch. There were no signs of a scuffle.

She hurried back home as Bill came downstairs. “Gretel has left”, Sandra said. “I think she may have followed one of those migratory flights at first light.”

“I am not surprised”, Bill replied. “With the goats and Hansel gone, there wasn’t much to keep her here.”

“Last evening was her way of saying goodbye to us!’ Sandra said. “We will miss her!” “But I’m glad she always felt free to fly and follow her own destination.

Free To Fly Epilogue

It was the next spring and all the snow had melted with no more ice on the pond. Bill and Sandra had sold the inn and were now in the new home they had built on the same side of the road as the barn. They no longer had a direct view of the pond but there was a stream that ran between the barn and their home on its way down to the river.

Bill had come in for lunch and looked out the kitchen window.

"Hey, Sandra, come look at this! There are six geese down by the stream!"

Sandra quickly came to the window. "Oh, Bill! That's Gretel and she is back with some friends. I'm going down there!"

As Sandra slowly approached them, one of the geese separated herself by a short distance from the others. As Sandra slowly moved closer, the cluster of geese seemed startled and all of them flew off.

Sandra came back to the house saying, "I am sure that is Gretel with the flock, and I don't have any corn to give them. I am going into town to buy some. They may come back and I want to be ready for them."

After her quick trip into town, she and Bill posted themselves at the window so they could see the stream. Later in the afternoon they saw the six geese return. As before, one of them separated slightly from the group.

Sandra took her corn and walked slowly toward them. As she came closer, the goose gave a flap to her wings. Sandra scattered her corn and walked away so the geese would not feel threatened. As she returned to the house, the lead goose began eating followed by the others. When they had eaten all the corn, Gretel gave one last wing flap and they all flew away.

As Sandra and Bill watched this touching moment they both had tears in their eyes as they realized this was very probably a last Goodbye.

Sandra expressed the feeling of both of them, saying, “I am so grateful she returned to let us know she had found her friends.

* * *

Gretel and her family have not returned,

but Sandra always had corn available.

Random Memories

Some of our different experiences popped into my head while writing all of this, but they didn't seem to fit with the chapters I was writing at the time. I let those ideas go, but now I think it is time for some random memories of this part of our life.

Early in our life in Vermont, actually about six months after moving in, we were doing some clean up in the front yard. It was probably on a Saturday; the weather was pleasant, and both Sandra and I were dressed in our work clothes. The front yard is short with the house rather close to the road. A car pulled to a stop on the road in front of the house, and the window rolled down. The driver stuck his head out of the window and said something. I walked closer to better hear him.

As I approached his car he asked, "Does this road go to Newfane?"

I paused a beat and responded in my best imitation of an old Vermonter accent, *"Nope. . . don't go no wheah. Jus stays theah!"*

I immediately broke into laughter, and explained to him that this was an expression I had heard in a story about local history, and had been waiting for the right time to use it. I apologized and did then give him proper directions for continuing on to the nearby town of Newfane.

* * *

We took the first opportunity we could after Sandra's return from Toledo following her Mother's funeral service. We had heard about the long ago former owner, who was the last dairy farmer in 1945, and Sandra had wanted to invite him for dinner. His name was Ransome Blood and he was still living in the area. Dave Berrie, our realtor, contacted him and extended the invitation. He hadn't been in the house since he left in 1945, and was pleased with the chance to see it again with all the changes Mr. McCall, the New York Banker, had made. We made it a small dinner party with Dave and his wife, Cindy.

Sandra arranged a nice dinner, and my only task was the fire in the fireplace. I had the good seasoned wood Brent had provided, and set it in the fireplace. Before the guests were to arrive, I opened the damper and lit the fire. Immediately, the dining room filled with smoke and then the living room. It turned out that the damper had already been open, apparently since before we bought the house, and I had just reversed the setting, closing off the ventilation. I was able to clear it out with a now open damper and open doors, so that our guests wouldn't walk through clouds of smoke. The pervading odor of the wood fire was enough for them to know what had happened. They were gracious enough not to comment on this newcomer and his fireplace skills.

Our guest of honor was thrilled with his tour of the house and delighted with the opportunity. He had recently had transplants of both knees, but bounded up and down the stairs. His bright eyes were sparkling, and it was such a treat for us to have him. That was the last time we saw Ransome Blood, and heard that he had passed away. Our timing was good for him and for us.

* * *

This is one of the cutest memories of our Inn time. Sandra and I were going to have a busy day so we were in the dining room before lunch, setting the table for the evening meal. I glanced out through the large triple door window, and saw a different sight beginning to happen in the backyard. We both became entranced as we watched the scene.

This was winter, snow covered the steep hill behind the Inn and the storage shed built into the hill. We had had a slight thaw and then more freezing, so the snow was crusty and slippery. When I had glanced outside, I saw a wild turkey emerge from the trees at the top of the snow covered slope. As we watched, we saw this was a full grown turkey hen with her little chicks. As the procession of mama, followed by her chicks, began walking single file down the slope to the shed roof, we counted fourteen of them. She, followed by her little ones, marched up over the roof peak and down to the edge. Mama paused at the edge and launched herself out and down to the ground. One by one the babies followed her, fluttering their little wings until landing.

Mama started walking, followed by her chicks in a in a line of one-by-one. She was headed for a large barberry bush that was loaded with bright red berries from the top about half way down. Mama began eating her way around the bush taking the berries she could reach. Some unseen, earlier, smaller creatures had already taken the lowest hanging ones. The little ones following her tried to eat berries, but were too short to reach them. They didn't give up easily, and treated us to one of the cleverest sights. These little chicks surrounding the bush began hopping vertically, and at the same time tried to stretch their necks and heads higher. After several attempts, they still couldn't reach the height of the remaining berries.

Mama decided she should move on, so she started walking across a side hill to get up to the old apple orchard. The chicks dutifully followed her, but had trouble walking across the slope. Mama had some trouble with her feet slipping out from under her because of the slippery snow. The little ones treated us to another funny view as all fourteen of them had the same problem of slipping. They would slip, lose their footing, and scrabble their way back up to where they were. Then they would go a few feet, slip again, until finally, they all reached the top of the hill and the apple orchard. Mama flew up to the top of the trees and spent some time eating the remains of the few frozen, spoiled apples still on the trees. The chicks could not fly so they waited down on the snow. She stayed in the trees until she finished what she wanted, flew down, gathered up her chicks, and they walked off single file out of our sight toward the heavy woods. That is a great memory, and was the last of our turkey sightings.

* * *

Sandra had quite an experience. It was just after our Inn Opening and the Fall Foliage business rush had ended. She had put in a demanding two week period of preparing meals and managing the Inn, and without exaggeration was exhausted. She had decided that it was necessary to get on top of everything, because we didn't really know what our business was going to be like. She decided to take the laundry into town rather than over use our washer and dryer, as well as go to recycling with our wine bottles and other materials. So she loaded up the car and started out. I, along with Darren, went out to the fields with the tractor to begin the fall clean up.

After an unknown period of time, an acquaintance pulled into the barnyard and signaled to me out in the field. I drove the tractor back to the barn to hear the news that Sandra had an accident and was being taken to the hospital. I jumped in his car with him and was given a ride, as he explained what he knew of the accident. Meanwhile Darren had to fix the flat tire on our truck. I will take the suspense out of the story to say that Sandra had been treated at the hospital and was pronounced bruised but nothing serious.

The actual accident, from reports by bystanders, was serious, and Sandra was truly fortunate to have survived with the minimal injury report. Here is the incident:

Sandra was driving on the main road into town. She remembers being very sleepy and looking for a pull-off so she could rest. She fell asleep before the point where the road curved, and she crossed over the center and into a swale. She continued along the path of the swale, and as it became deeper the swale passed through a culvert under a driveway. Luckily, just before the culvert, the car followed the uphill slope next to the culvert and went airborne. In the air, the car turned upside down and landed on its top; then it flipped back to land on its wheels. It proceeded down-hill, nose first, knocking over some small trees before coming to a stop. Sandra had been so tired that she slept through the entire episode. Fortunately, an observer saw the entire incident, as she was standing outside for a cigarette break, and ran right back to her office and called 911.

Thinking about this, it is possible being asleep kept Sandra relaxed and allowed her to avoid serious harm. Looking at the car afterwards, it was totaled, and it seemed miraculous that her only injury was a severe pain from the seatbelt over her chest.

* * *

I wrote about Brent early in this memoir when he returned the extra $5.00 I had paid for firewood, and I mentioned him later, when I included the brief part about splitting fire wood. One day, I believe it was not long after we had sold the Inn, and (had some money), he came to see me accompanied by a younger man I had been casually acquainted with. They were wondering if I could loan them enough money to buy a piece of equipment used for splitting wood for their business. First, to understand Vermont, you need to know that wood stoves are a way of life. There is always a market for wood; and wood is a renewable energy source. These two guys had teamed together.

The equipment they wanted to buy was large. I forget the name, but will describe it. It was a one-person operating machine with a rack, that would accept several twenty feet long logs, with a conveyor belt that would move a single log to a cutting position. The operator would then actuate a chain saw that would cut the long log into the desired length for a wood stove. The cut lengths would roll into a station to be automatically split. These pieces would fall onto a conveyor belt that was positioned to carry them up and dump them into the truck for delivery to the customer's home. One of these guys would operate the splitting equipment and the other would do the delivery. The multiplier effect of this equipment would allow them to split up to ten cords a day, and be far more efficient.

This was an expensive purchase costing roughly $30,000. I knew Brent, and from his reputation he seemed reliable. I didn't know his associate, Travis, other than he was a recent high school graduate, had had a serious injury, and was personable. I was impressed with their "ask for the order" mentality, but felt loaning them money without any collateral would be too risky. So I prepared a rental agreement for them to sign with a monthly payment schedule, bought the equipment and they were in business. Unfortunately, the younger man didn't have the same level of business ethics as Brent, and pulled out of the business without looking back. Brent decided he would operate alone and continued paying the full monthly amount. He kept this going, and after final payment of the full amount of the original purchase price plus prevailing market interest rates, I signed the equipment over to him. It was a pleasure being involved with him.

* * *

Another man that I was always impressed with was Chris Williams, who also lived in the village. Chris operated an auto repair business out of his garage at his home. But to describe Chris in this way is not adequate. He could do anything mechanical, and in my mind, was one of the most talented men to ever work with his hands and brain; a truly logical person. Not to describe everything he did, but he plowed our driveways in the winter, helped with haying in the summer, repaired our truck, welded broken parts whenever needed, and did whatever he needed to fit a schedule that met his customer's needs. When we eventually moved away, he bought our tractor and equipment on a payment schedule that he met faithfully with a check in the mail every month until complete.

* * *

When we built our new house, we placed it on a one acre portion of the full 17 acres I have referred to. This was at the far edge of the entire 115 acres we had originally purchased. This one acre piece was bordered on the one side with a fence that ran from the road all the way down to the river. The interesting fact about this was that the land, just on the other side of the fence, had been a small cemetery at one time. As a part of this, there was a majestic old maple tree that stood on a raised ground area at the edge of what had been the cemetery. The roots of this tree had grown around what had been a small morgue dug into the raised ground area. In those olden days of digging graves by hand shovel, the frozen ground made it necessary to keep bodies until the spring thaw. The morgue under the tree was used for body storage and, of course, was no longer used.

At some time in local history, date unknown to me, the bodies in the cemetery were exhumed and moved to a new cemetery across the river on what is known as Depot Road. Apparently, when the move occurred, the grave monument for the founder of our village, Williamsville, was left on our property. The trees grew in around the monument and it wasn't until we built our house that I discovered it.

The monument was in the shape of an obelisk and was engraved with the names of John Williams and his descendants. The base was separate and I found it in the nearby trees. I had the idea of moving this monument and its base down to the village and installing it in front of the Old Grange Hall that was used for Town Meetings. I requested permission of the Town Planning Commission because of zoning requirements. They approved, so I arranged the move and installation.

* * *

That brings to mind another brief experience when we had to install our temporary septic system. This was out on the side yard where, coincidentally, there was a rough, hewn granite post that was next to the road. We had a visit from one of the Town Selectmen that told us we couldn't do any development out there because of the grave stone, and this was sacred burial ground. We were able to convince him it was an old hitching post and not a grave stone, especially since it was right next to the road.

* * *

At the time we placed the Inn on the real estate market, I began to have some extra time, so I applied for an open position on the Town Planning Commission. Fortunately, the Town, though geographically covering about 29 square miles, had a population of only 1500. Occasionally, there could be minor controversy, but I can't recall anything of substance. The makeup of the Commission began to change with normal attrition, and the new members seemed to be changing to more of a liberal mindset. At the same time, the State began to require that all towns prepare a Town Plan that should meet State directives, that to my mind furthered the liberal mentality. As we set about writing the Town Plan, it became obvious I had become a minority on the Planning Commission. I still remember my resignation comment, "I feel like the kid in the playground on the wrong end of the teeter-totter."

* * *

Another incident in public life provided a good experience. Elections were being held and there was one open position for someone from our Town. This was for a Regional High School Board and would be replacing Dave Berrie, the realtor who had sold us the Inn property those years earlier. Dave had reached the end of his term and felt good about the Board, so I decided to apply. Without any competition this was an easy election. I took on the practical role of saving money by changing the high school heating system. This was an old system of electrical heating that created expensive heating bills, and were projected by the Power Company to increase every year. We did a study that evaluated alternative methods, and recommended a change that would seriously reduce costs. This new heating system would use wood chips, and while radical to many, had examples of other school's usage that justified it. The first public vote failed, so we brought it up for another later vote. We were better prepared for this vote and it passed. The conversion took place and the heating results justified the change.

* * *

Sandra and I had been in our new house for two years, when we decided to take a driving trip down to see our friends, Shel and Olivia, in Florida. Our travel plan included a stop to see friends in North Carolina, then overnight in either Charleston or Savannah before going on to be with Shel and Olivia in Palm Beach Gardens. We would also visit Walt Disney World and on the return trip would use the Amtrak Car Train to Washington, D.C. before driving back home.

This was where our life began to change again, and was the beginning of the end for this memoir of our life in Vermont.

During our trip south, we visited Savannah; and we fell in love again. The community we toured was The Landings on Skidaway Island. The ancient live oak trees, draped with Spanish moss, lagoons, golf courses, tennis courts, the ocean, colonial Savannah and the mild weather all combined to sell us on living there. Laurie and Darren were well established in Vermont. Jon and Elena were also established in New Jersey. We had a large house with high taxes, cold and snow. Why not move on? We made our decision to buy a spec house that overlooked a lagoon and was within walking distance of a marina for a boat we thought about buying. We signed the papers and had a house. After the closing, we made arrangements with the Landings Developer to manage rentals of our new house for us until we could sell our Vermont house and finally move down.

* * *

On the drive back north we called Laurie to invite her and Darren for dinner when we got home. Our intention was to break our news. It was dinner time and the two of them arrived at the door with Laurie carrying the balloons to announce her first pregnancy. All of us were shocked when we heard the other news, but finally accepted this would work out. The next years before actually moving were a great period for us.

Our first granddaughter, Danielle, was born, and Sandra and I had a perfect two years of providing care for her during the week as Laurie and Darren worked at their jobs. We had a special second birthday for Danielle. Jon and Elena had come to visit with their daughter, Alexa, who was five months younger than Danielle. At the same time, we were so lucky that our niece, Amy (Krueger) and her husband, Joe Marsh, with their daughter, Eleanore, had stopped on their way back home to Pittsburgh. Eleanore was also age two, so we had a grand tea party for the girls.

* * *

I had listed our house for sale with our original realtor, Dave, and prepared a glossy brochure patterned after the Sotheby brochure from our Inn. We did have some lookers, but the real estate market was going into the doldrums. Meanwhile the market was good at our new Landings community and we were able to rent out our new home to folks who were building their own home. We had three different tenants, using the community real estate group as property managers, and over this period we had good care with a slight net plus income.

* * *

Our time arrived. Dave's former real estate partner brought back a local Vermont prospect to look at our home again. The time was right for them to buy, and they agreed this would be a perfect home for their two daughters. We were very pleasantly surprised when we were told who the buyers were. The Doctor who had delivered Danielle would be living in our house.

* * *

We could now leave Vermont and end our involvement of the past thirteen years with this property and the life it had brought us. As a couple, we had learned to face many challenges and keep our good humor. Our life was not always easy, and we had arguments, but we always resolved whatever differences we might have. I can say that even though the actual Inn operation was not financially successful; the personal satisfaction for both of us was extremely rewarding, and we would not have changed our original decision.

* * *

I don’t know how to answer the question: Would we do it again?

Epilogue

It was now seventeen years after we had moved south from Vermont. Laurie, Darren and family had moved farther north and were living in Richmond, Vermont. Danielle has a brother, Connor, who was born three years after Danielle and is now in his first year at the University of Florida. Danielle had become a mother with a son, Kaiden, who became our first great grandson.

As an entirely separate addition to this Epilogue and one that is being written some years later, Danielle and her husband Zach Martindale, live in Maryland, and have just given birth to our great granddaughter, Paige. As a further update, Jon and Elena live in Kearny, NJ. Their daughter, Alexa, has graduated from City University of New York and is now working at The Metropolitan Museum. Her brother, Sean, four years younger is in his senior year of high school and is scouting for a College.

Sandra and I had traveled from our home in Ocala, Florida to spend a week in Vermont, and to see Kaiden for the first time. It was a fine visit and Laurie took some time off from her work. One of the treats for us was her chauffeuring of us back to visit Williamsville which was the location of our former Inn, home and property. It was an exciting return for us.

The house that was the Inn had been sold again, and there was no one home so we could not meet the new owners. We could see from the outside that they had made changes to enhance the building. As a former owner, with pride in all the changes I had made, I found everything they had done highly positive. We regretted not meeting them.

The barn had some significant changes. The current owner was in the barn so we had a chance for him to tour us. This was the second owner since we had left and both had made changes. The silo had been removed and a house had been attached to the back corner of the barn by the first owner. The current owner had fully renovated the barn by replacing the roofing, windows and moving a large sliding door from the front wall to the end closest to the driveway. The inside had major renovation, with removal of all the horse stalls, addition of a first-class wood working shop and other leisure uses. Simply, all of these changes were top of the line.

We also stopped at the house we had built, and had the pleasure of meeting all the members of the family that bought from us. The daughters were now in university and were home for a visit. The mother was an author and was having a very small cabin built that she planned to use as her writing retreat. This was being sited very close to the position where I had originally found the grave monument of the founder of Williamsville.

I felt a separate source of pleasure: Before we had sold the house, about 20 years ago, I had planted some trees. The maples had grown very well and were in Fall color for us. I had also planted six walnut trees in the form of walnuts, still in their shells, along the bank of the stream bed. I was so pleased to see that five of the six had grown, were healthy, and served as guardians of that edge of the property.

We said goodbye to this former life, probably for the last time.

Creating a Country Inn

The End

APPENDIX

Rules and Policies

At various points within this memoir, I have included our perspective on specific aspects of Inn Keeping I believe should be carefully thought through by anyone considering entering into this business. They are not necessarily profound; in fact, having been through the experience of both creating and operating an Inn, I believe they are common sense. Of course, I can say that now since we are no longer in the business.

If I/We were that good, we wouldn't have had to learn so much from doing. All of this would have been obvious before we started. Since we were not that good about predicting all of this, I thought that anyone interested in reading this book might find benefit in having it all laid out in one place. This chapter is being presented as an Appendix includes the Rules placed within the memoir followed by a listing of the various Inn Policies we developed.

The following are these ***Rules:***

> *It is probably somewhat more rare than not, to find or create an opportunity to begin an Inn or B&B in the location where you are now living. There are, of course, those that are currently living in a large home or can find a large home to buy. This is more so for a B&B than an Inn. The simple definitions we are using in this book consider an Inn as one that will provide meals beyond breakfast. This generally requires a larger and more equipped kitchen and greater lounging/reception area. You may also assume a greater number of guest rooms.*

Recognize that you may have to uproot yourself in order to find the opportunity and move to an area that is new. With that, you have to face what is a new life in a new location at the same time as beginning a new career. This is quite achievable, but if you have been comfortable living in the same home for some time the personal challenges may be difficult. Try to understand yourself and how you react to totally new things as you are making a decision on the business of inn keeping.

Inn keeping is a very busy life and if pleasure activities are most important to you, you might want to carefully consider what you are taking on. Time off from the Inn for personal reasons becomes a rare occurrence.

If you are terrified by new things, think long and hard about your decision.

If it is at all possible, try to time your beginning in the best weather in your climate. In our case, Winter in Vermont was always harsh. Stated simply, it could be very cold, windy, and snowy.

Expect the unexpected.

Pay particular attention to all rules and regulations, Local, State and Federal that will apply to the business you intend to operate. This will apply not only to an existing hospitality industry business, but to any rules or regulations that may be required if you are converting from one zoning classification to another.

This is a responsibility you must assume. You cannot assume that a real estate broker will bring all pertinent regulations to your attention, without specifically requesting the information and/or advice for your consideration. You must ask. Before signing a purchase contract prepared, ask your attorney to review this for all applicable Laws, Regulations and/or Permits that will apply.

Since your project will eventually require specific final approvals, such as Health Inspection, Fire Inspection, etc., invite the involved State, Local, or even Federal key personnel to meet you at your project early on in the project. You will gain immeasurably from this effort, both in the personal touch of meeting them as well as gaining an understanding of any particular requirements they are sensitive to.

Be prepared for anything, keep your wits about you and look for common sense solutions.

Reach out to anyone who can possibly assist you in developing your market personality, and where possible to refer business to you. This does not necessarily require you to spend money on advertising, but it also does not mean you should not advertise. It means, develop your personality so that you benefit from personal referrals and word-of-mouth. If you have a Bed and Breakfast, be sure you are referring guests to restaurants, and that those restaurants know you are interested in them and will return the favor.

The decision to offer complimentary wine is one to consider carefully. As I have written, that offering is what we did, but there is no question in my mind that it definitely caused us to sell less wine from the list. It is natural that any free wine will encourage guests to accept the offering, and not go on to view other wines that were available and affordable. A suggestion is to offer a complimentary glass of wine before dinner, and have all dinner wines priced on the List. If you are offering a Wine List with priced wines, please investigate your local regulations regarding the need for a license to serve with your meals.

Establish a policy that is always invoked at time of accepting reservations. Ask if any of the Guests have any dietary considerations the Inn should be aware of for any meals or snacks. Be as specific as possible. It can become very embarrassing if this is not determined until after food is placed on the table.

Start making reservations for yourself at Inns or B&Bs and make a practice of meeting as many of the guests as possible. Have conversations and learn about them and how they selected the B&B you are in. What are their plans while they are there? Learn as much as you can from your Hosts. Obviously, you do not want to become a nuisance, but you can be subtle; and you will benefit greatly.

Be aware that there may be times when you have your family members and/or good friends as guests at the same time you have other guests. It will be natural to have the situation when you as inn keepers may not be able to be with your close family/friends as you will be performing your role as host to paying guests. It can be a sensitive time regarding familial relationships. It could be a situation when you as inn keeper can be emotional or it could be a family member who is expecting a greater personal relationship than you can give at the time.

When committing yourself to a major production, such as a wedding, reception or some other major social function, be sure the method of payment is checked thoroughly. And investigate the parties in advance to determine their reliability. If you are tying up your Inn for a particular occasion, obtain references and secure a substantial deposit. In these days of scams, you cannot be too careful.

Inn Policies should be prepared to cover most aspects of owning and operating an Inn or B&B. It is easy to overlook the work of preparation, but as an earlier rule says: "Expected the Unexpected." It is better to have thought out some of the many possibilities and have some idea of how your response should be guided.

Inn Policies

We had decided that we should attempt to establish **Inn Policies** that could give us guidance on key matters. There were no guidelines available that we were aware of so, we created our policies as we became aware of anything that could be significant. As you look over these policies you will see some are individually specific and may not be suitable for the style of your Inn. These should be considered as guidelines.

The policy that was most innovative and popular with our part time employees is the incentive plan included in Compensation. This was most helpful in keeping these employees on the payroll. Policies should be reviewed and changed when Inn Keepers agree.

One example of a major change in our policies, was in the days when meals would be provided. We found that our original policy of providing evening dinner every day was applying too much pressure on us as Inn Keepers. Naturally, the pressure was much greater on my Wife/Chef. During our early days we found our expectation of business was unrealistic, and we had too many days when our Inn Guests were too infrequent to support the expense of maintaining supplies on hand to meet dinner menus. Also the pressure on the kitchen staff to be constantly on call was unrealistic. The policy on meals as we changed it is included in the table below:

The policies we established are listed in alphabetical order.

Accounts Payable

All accounts due are to be paid within 20 days of receipt

unless otherwise shown with a date due.

Alcoholic beverages

All alcoholic beverages for sale to be purchased from

authorized dealers.

Recommended dealer sales price to be shown on Wine List.

Wine List to be reviewed each month prior to dealer visit.

Bath Robes

All bath robes to be checked after each visit to determine if used.

If robe is used, must be laundered.

After laundry, robe to be prepared for hanging in guest rooms.

Compensation

Inn Keepers receive monthly compensation equal to minimum wage.

Full time employees to receive amount determined by Inn Keeper and agreed to by employees. Each employee may be different from other employees.

Part time employees will share in incentive compensation determined by Inn Keepers.

Incentive compensation to be calculated based on amount contributed by Inn Keepers as described herein. The amount of $1.00 per room day will be deducted from the room revenue paid by guests and will be held in escrow by Inn Keepers for a period of 3 months. At the conclusion of the 3 month period the total dollar amount will be distributed to employees, based on the percentage of hours each worked over the period.

Contractors

List of approved contractors will be maintained by Inn Keepers.

Approval of Contractors will be at discretion of Inn Keepers.

Employment of Contractors may only be approved by Inn Keepers.

Cross Country trail equipment may only be operated by Inn Keeper or Employee approved by Inn Keeper.

Cross Country Ski Trails

Changes to cross country ski trail system may only be made by Inn Keeper

Employees

Inn Keepers are considered full time employees.

Employees whose primary jobs are working within the

interior of the Inn, mainly rooms and kitchen are part time. Employees who work a combination of outside and inside for occasional book keeping are considered full time.

Farm Equipment

All farm equipment is to be stored at the barn and is not considered to be used for any activity considered to be inn keeping.

All fields are not considered to be any part of the inn.

Fire Places and Wood Stoves

Fireplaces and wood stoves are to be used for wood burning only.

Fireplaces and wood stoves are to be used only with screens and/or doors in place.

Fireplaces and wood stoves are to be cleaned each day after usage.

Guests

All guests are to be registered with names and addresses.

At time of reservation, guests are to be asked if they have any dietary restrictions.

Any dietary restrictions are to be entered in guest reservation sheet.

Guests under age 12 are not encouraged.

Horses

Horses are not part of the Inn.

Horses are not to be used for any inn related activity.

Laundry

The laundry is used for all Inn washable goods.

Inn laundry may also be washed in commercially available laundries at discretion of Inn Keeper.

Inn laundry may also be used for laundry of guest or employee goods with approval of Inn Keeper.

Meals

Dinner will be served every Friday and Saturday.

Dinner will be served every day during holiday weeks of Christmas, New Year, Presidents Day and Fall Foliage

Dinner on other days may be negotiated by Inn Keepers.

Dinners, unless otherwise changed by Inn Keepers will be served at 7:30 p.m.

Dinners will be a fixed menu determined by Chef.

Breakfast meals will be served every day from 7:00 to 9:00 a.m.

Pets

Pets, other than those owned by Inn Keepers, are not permitted within

Interior of the Inn.

Pond

The pond is not a part of the Inn, and is not to be used for wading or swimming.

Reservations

Reservations are accepted for all days the Inn is open and space is available.

Children under age 12 are not accepted.

Multiple day stay duration may be required during peak business periods for specific activities. Inn Keepers will discuss at time of reservation request.

Room Rates

Room rates will be posted for reservations clerks to reference.

Room rates may be variable by room and date.

Rooms

All rooms have private baths.

Rooms vary with bed size: King, Queen, Double, Twin

Smoking

The Country Inn is a non-smoking facility.

Time-Off

Employees may have time-off with advance notice preferred.

Vacation

Time-off policy applies.

Weddings

The Inn encourages weddings, but specific requirements apply.

Discuss among Inn Keepers before committing.

Creating a Country Inn

Picture Portfolio

First look at the house. Our first visit.

After renovation. Opening Day sign.

Back view of Country Inn after all renovations.

Yes, we do have snow.
Fire escape and firewood shed.

View out in back. See turkey story.

Country Inn entrance from parking area.

The first view of the barn.

Winter scene of pond and fields.
From our favorite wedding.

The path that Sandra carried food &
water for Hansel & Gretel led past the barn.

View from field past horse
pasture to Inn on other side of road.

The swimming hole down where the river bends

Dining Room with table/chairs,
antique corner cabinet from England.

Living Room

Sandra, Inn Keeper and Chef, in her kitchen.

Bill, Inn Keeper and Garcon, at work.

Soul Mates

Illustrations

from

Free To Fly

Hansel

Gretel

Wimble

Cautious Friends